# BOXING'S
# STRANGEST
## FIGHTS

*Other titles in this series*

Soccer's Strangest Matches    Andrew Ward
Cricket's Strangest Matches    Andrew Ward
Horse-Racing's Strangest Races    Andrew Ward

# BOXING'S
# STRANGEST
## FIGHTS

## GRAEME KENT

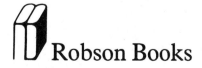
Robson Books

FIRST PUBLISHED IN GREAT BRITAIN IN 1991
BY ROBSON BOOKS LTD, BOLSOVER HOUSE,
5–6 CLIPSTONE STREET, LONDON W1P 7EB

Copyright © 1991 Graeme Kent
The right of Graeme Kent to be identified as author of this
work has been asserted by him in accordance with the
Copyright, Designs and Patents Act 1988

**British Library Cataloguing in Publication Data**
Kent, Graeme
    Boxing's strangest fights.
    1. Boxing – Biographies – Collections
    I. Title
    796.830922

    ISBN 0 86051 715 2

Photoset in North Wales by
Derek Doyle & Associates, Mold, Clwyd
Printed in Great Britain by
Butler & Tanner Ltd, London and Frome

# *Contents*

# *Introduction*

Boxing attracts eccentrics. Perhaps you have to be a little crazy to have anything to do with the ring. There is great richness in its history and folklore, and I hope that I have done some justice to it in these pages.

I have been drawn to boxing and its legends ever since my sporting grandmother told me that she once felt the biceps of Freddy Welsh, later to be the world lightweight champion, when he was just starting out in the game in Pontypridd in 1905.

Several years earlier that same grandmother had served a whisky and water to Buffalo Bill Cody when he had ridden over from his touring Wild West Show to Tintern, where she was working as a barmaid. I never felt quite the same awe for the Buffalo Bill connection as I did about the one with Freddy Welsh.

In compiling the stories for this collection I have drawn upon many printed sources, but I have also gone to as many primary sources as possible. The task took me so long that many of the fighters and followers of the game who were so generous with their time and friendship are no longer with us.

I would like to thank T B Shepherd, compiler of the best of all boxing anthologies, *The Noble Art*. 'Shep' spent many years as a schoolmaster in the tough King's Cross area of London and taught a number of schoolboys who later became professional champions – Danny and Dickie O'Sullivan, Terry Allen, and many others. Through him I met such ring luminaries as Danny O'Sullivan, the former bantamweight champion of Great Britain and a considerable raconteur in his own right.

From an older generation I am indebted to the memories of Johnny Cuthbert, featherweight and lightweight champion of Great Britain in the 1920s, who provided a fund of stories about boxing in this country between the wars.

Vic Hardwicke, the boxing statistician, came to my aid with details of the Monocled Boxer, Desmond Jeans, and is just one of the followers of the sport to whom I owe a debt.

Above all I am grateful to all those former boxers, champions and non-champions, who have spent so much time talking to me about the sport they practised with such courage and distinction. If the total time I have spent listening to their anecdotes about the ring were added up it would amount to quite a slice of my life. The rest I have probably wasted.

# The Gentle Sex

## London, June 1722

Organized boxing is generally considered to have got under way in Great Britain in 1719, when James Figg, the first heavyweight champion, opened his boxing academy, known as Figg's Amphitheatre.

Within three years women were also trying to get in on the act. It started with an advertisement in a London newspaper.

### Challenge

I, Elizabeth Wilkinson, of Clerkenwell, having had some words with Hannah Hyfield, and requiring satisfaction, do invite her to meet me upon the stage, and box me for three guineas; each woman holding half-a-crown in her hand, and the first woman that drops the money to lose the battle.

Hannah Hyfield was just as spirited, because within a few days her reply appeared in the same journal.

### Answer

I, Hannah Hyfield, of Newgate Market, hearing of the resoluteness of Elizabeth Wilkinson, will not fail, God willing, to give her more blows than words – desiring home blows, and from her, no favour: she may expect a good thumping!

The projected match attracted a great deal of attention, but it never came off. The authorities clamped down upon the proposed meeting with great firmness. Both would-be contestants were informed that such an encounter would violate both public decency and ethics. If Elizabeth and Hannah attempted to go ahead with their bout they would both be thrown into prison.

The contest was cancelled.

# The Boys from Bristol

## Hailsham, Sussex, October 1805

A number of well-known boxers have ended their careers in prison. John Gully was the first champion to begin his fighting life there.

He was the son of a Bristol butcher. In 1805, Gully found himself a prisoner in the King's Bench prison for debt. While he was there he achieved something of a reputation as a fighter when he thrashed the prison bully.

News of the fighting debtor reached the ears of another Bristolian, Hen Pearce, better known as the 'Game Chicken', the bare-knuckle champion of England. Pearce visited Gully in the King's Bench and suggested that they have a friendly set-to with the mufflers.

Gully acquitted himself so well in the sparring session that Pearce recommended him to a well-known patron of the prize-ring, Fletcher Read.

Read paid off Gully's debts on the understanding that the young West Country man embark upon a career as a prize-fighter. Gully was not reluctant, but after an initial training period he was aghast when told that in his first professional contest he had been matched against his benefactor, Hen Pearce, the champion of England.

The two men met shortly before the battle of Trafalgar was fought, at Hailsham, before a huge crowd. The Duke of Clarence, later William IV, watched the bout from horseback at the rear of the crowd.

The contest lasted sixty-four rounds, a total period of one hour and seventeen minutes. Gully put up a tremendous fight, but the experience of the champion was too much for him and he was forced to retire. After he had thrown in the sponge, Pearce came over and shook his hand.

'You're a damned good fellow,' said the Game Chicken. 'I'm hard put to it to stand. You're the only man that ever stood up to me.'

Pearce retired from the ring and John Gully was generally accepted as the new champion. He fought only twice more, each time against the Lancashire giant, John Gregson. In their first encounter, near Newmarket, Gully knocked his opponent out in thirty-six rounds.

The first contest had been so desperately close that the two men were matched again. They met at Woburn, on 10 May 1808. The match attracted so much interest that it was said would-be spectators occupied every spare bed, stable and barn between London and Woburn. One local landlord charged fifteen customers two guineas a head to lie on chairs or on the floor.

The press grew so strong that rumours circulated that the French had invaded. The Dunstable Volunteers turned out in full fighting array, only to receive the disappointing news that the crowd had only assembled to witness a match with the bare knuckles.

Gully won the second contest in eight rounds and immediately announced his retirement from the ring. He became an innkeeper and a bookmaker. In this way he assembled a great fortune, bought a colliery and ran a string of racehorses. He even became Member of Parliament for Pontefract. He died at the age of eighty in 1863, having won the Derby three times and sired twenty-four children.

Hen Pearce, the other Bristol boy, who had defeated Gully and launched him on his career, died in poverty at the age of thirty-two.

# *All to See a Fight!*

## Hayes, May 1817

Fight fans have always been ready to put themselves out for the pleasure of seeing a scrap. At the beginning of the 19th century, when the sport was illegal, followers of boxing needed to be almost as fit and enterprising as the fighters themselves in order to achieve their aim.

On 26 May 1817, more than 30,000 would-be spectators turned out in dreadful weather to see Jack Scroggins meet Ned Turner in a field near Hayes in Middlesex. These hardy enthusiasts were prepared to pay three shillings a head and brave the pickpockets, muggers and assorted low life attracted by the easy pickings of such occasions.

It was estimated that more than 8000 carriages choked all approaches to the field for miles in every direction. So dense was the throng that those spectators closest to the ring were shoved forward, swamping the fighting area. This brought the bout to a halt.

Despite all the efforts of the former prize-fighters acting as stewards to clear the ring with their horse-whips, no space could be regained for the contest to continue. Finally the bout was called off.

To avoid a riot it was decided to move the whole assemblage three miles to the north to Hillingdon, near Uxbridge, where – so it was announced optimistically – a bout between two other prize-fighters, Randall and Dick, would be held.

Practically every one of the 30,000 determined fight fans in the crowd doggedly set off across country in heavy rain. Some were on foot, others on horseback, while the rest followed down the lanes and across fields in a variety of horse-drawn vehicles.

The vast, excited concourse arrived at Hillingdon, to be greeted with the news that the local magistrates had banned the proposed contest between Randall and Dick.

The rain was still pouring down, the fields had been churned into mud and the spectators had been milling around for hours without food or rest. Few of them were put off. There was news of a third possible contest, between Holt and O'Donnell, to be held near Hounslow Heath, some five miles to the south.

Still in their thousands, the walkers, the riders, the traps and the coaches headed south. It was five-thirty in the afternoon before they reached the heath. Most of them had been on the move since dawn.

At last they were rewarded. Holt and O'Donnell duly turned out and performed to the satisfaction of the doughty followers of the sport.

# Fighting the Devil

## Nottingham, July 1835

Many fighters have had their work cut out giving away weight to an opponent. Some have used superior skill to outwit their adversary. Others have tried to talk their way out of trouble.

When William Thompson, otherwise known as Bendigo, fought the former gamekeeper Ben Caunt at Appleby House near Nottingham in 1835, the sprightly bare-knuckle fighter was giving away forty pounds in weight and six inches in height.

It became apparent that Caunt was likely to smother him with his powerful rushes unless he could think of something very quickly. In those days a round came to an end when a fighter was knocked to the ground. He then had sixty seconds in which to recover and come back to the mark.

Bendigo hit upon the idea of going down every time the giant even touched him with a punch. Consequently some of the rounds lasted only a few seconds.

Caunt and his backers were screaming at the smaller man to stand and fight. Bendigo would merely smile and go down again. This was Caunt's first real bout in the prize-ring and he did not know how to cope with the elusive tactics of his adversary.

When he was not going to ground and winking up at his enraged opponent, Bendigo was busily engaged in jeering at Caunt and throwing every sort of insult at him.

Eventually the younger fighter could stand it no longer. At

the end of the twenty-second round he followed Bendigo to the latter's corner. While Bendigo was sitting on his second's knee, as was the custom between rounds, Caunt hit him with a mighty punch.

The giant was at once disqualified and Bendigo's backers won their bets. Much later, after his retirement from the ring and no fewer than twenty-eight sojourns in prison, Bendigo was converted, and became an itinerant preacher. One day he met an old acquaintance. Smugly the old fighter told his friend that these days he was fighting the devil.

'Indeed,' said the other man coolly. 'Then I hope you're fighting him a damned sight fairer than you fought Ben Caunt, or all my sympathies will be with Satan!'

# Seconds Out!

## Boston Corners, October 1853

The first bare-knuckle fighters in the early days of the American prize-ring were a hard and unpleasant lot. Two of the roughest were John Morrissey and Yankee Sullivan. When they met in 1853, a violent struggle was forecast, but no one expected the crazy free-for-all which ensued.

Both men came from Ireland but made their homes in the USA. Morrissey was born in Tipperary but moved to Troy, New York, when he was three years old. He developed into a hulking youth and worked at a variety of labouring jobs and on the river boats. He also became the leader of a gang of delinquents and on several occasions was convicted of robbery and assault.

Morrissey achieved a degree of local notoriety when he engaged in a brawl in a New York saloon known as the Empire Club. His adversary was a ruffian called Tom McCann. In the course of the struggle McCann knocked over a coal stove, spilling the embers all over the floor. In desperation he hurled Morrissey on top of the red-hot coals and held him down. After a while the unlookers doused the flames and Morrissey threw McCann off. The back of his coat was smoking. Ignoring the pain, he knocked the other man out before shrugging off the smouldering garment. For the rest of his life John Morrissey was known as Old Smoke.

He took up prize-fighting in California after he had failed to make his fortune in the gold rush there. In 1851, he was matched at Mare Island with an English fighter, George Thompson, who had just won the Californian championship. Thompson easily outboxed the American, but Morrissey's followers threatened the Englishman with revolvers until he committed a deliberate foul in order to be disqualified.

Morrissey returned to New York to follow his new twin careers of prize-fighter and opportunist. Soon he found himself matched with Yankee Sullivan.

Sullivan was even more villainous than Morrissey but not as cunning. He was born near Cork but as a young man was transported to Botany Bay in Australia for theft. He escaped by stowing away in a boat carrying cargo to New York. For a time he scraped a living as a bare-knuckle fighter and earned enough to open a disreputable saloon in the Bowery.

Gradually, Sullivan and Morrissey built up their reputations as the best fighters in the USA. It was inevitable that they should meet. Contracts were signed at an angry meeting in a New York saloon in September 1853. Each man backed himself for a thousand dollars.

The venue selected was a field about a quarter of a mile from the railway station of the small town of Boston Corners, about a hundred miles north of New York City. It had the great advantage of being situated at the meeting point of Massachusetts, Connecticut and the Empire State. No one was sure who had jurisdiction over this unimportant corner, making it less likely that the police would interfere.

The bout took place on a Wednesday afternoon before a crowd of about 5000. There was heavy betting on the outcome, with Morrissey being the declared favourite. He was thirty pounds heavier and three inches taller than his forty-one-year-old opponent, who also happened to be suffering from syphilis.

Before the bout Morrissey prowled around the ring, offering to bet $1000 to $800 on himself. He looked so confident that there were no takers.

Yet to the surprise and delight of most of the onlookers, the dour Sullivan had the best of the earlier rounds. He hit the bigger man at will and chased him about the ring, allowing

Morrissey no peace. Morrissey's backers grew ominously silent when it appeared that the favourite was going to be beaten by his older opponent.

In the thirty-seventh round Morrissey took Sullivan by the throat and started throttling him on the ropes. The crowd went wild and threatened to invade the ring at the sight of such chicanery. After a moment the seconds of both fighters poured into the roped square and started hitting one another. They were followed by hundreds of enraged spectators.

Frantically the timekeeper tried to get the bout under way again in the confusion. He shouted above the din, ordering both men to come up to scratch for the thirty-eighth round.

Morrissey heard him and broke away from the general rough-house to obey the official, toeing the line scratched in the centre of the ring. Sullivan was not so fortunate. He was so engrossed in punching Morrissey's second, Orville 'Awful' Gardner, that he did not hear the timekeeper's instructions.

The official gave Sullivan an extra thirty seconds to abandon his private fight and resume the official one. But Sullivan was still somewhere in the bowels of the furious crowd wreaking havoc on 'Awful' Gardner, and remained deaf to the announcement from the ring.

Morrissey's umpire promptly demanded that Sullivan be declared the loser as he had not come up to scratch. The official agreed and declared Morrissey the winner. The victor was hustled away through the crowd of milling spectators before anyone could realize what had happened.

The verdict in favour of Morrissey was yet another black mark on the record of prize-fighting in the USA. Both participants were arrested for engaging in an illegal bout. Sullivan was gaoled for a week before friends put up $1500 bail. Later Morrissey was given the choice of a $1200 fine or sixteen months in gaol. He chose to pay up.

The two boxers had contrasting fortunes after their bout at Boston Corners. Morrissey won the undisputed American championship when he defeated John Heenan in 1858. Commodore Vanderbilt, the wealthy railway magnate, became a friend and patron, helping him to amass a fortune. Morrissey operated a gambling hall, founded Saratoga racetrack, was elected to Congress, representing the Fifth New York District for two terms, and was then voted into the Senate. He became ill and died at the age of forty-seven.

Yankee Sullivan went West, embarking upon a career of crime in San Francisco. With his usual poor timing, he chose to do so at a period when the Vigilantes were beginning to clean up the city. He was arrested and placed overnight in a cell. The next morning he was found dead, the victim, it was rumoured, of a summary execution.

# The Rough-and-Tumble Champion

## New York, February 1855

John Morrissey claimed the title of champion of the USA after his defeat of Yankee Sullivan. Yet there were many who denied him even the claim of being the toughest man in New York.

One of these was Bill Poole, a former butcher who now kept a saloon and was emerging as a political leader. Poole considered the prize-ring a refuge for those of an effeminate nature. He gloried in the mantle of the rough-and-tumble champion of New York.

It was inevitable that Poole and Morrissey would clash. They belonged to different political factions, and anyway, New York was not big enough for two such strong-willed and fiery characters.

They met for $500 a side in an 'anything goes' contest at the Amos Street Dock. The roofs and windows of the adjacent buildings were packed with hundreds of eager spectators. Poole's gang got there first, before seven in the morning on a bitterly cold day. A little later Morrissey came swaggering down the street at the head of a crowd of heavily armed supporters.

At once Poole's gang closed in on Morrissey's followers. There was a pitched battle in the street. Morrissey's men came off the worse. They were beaten up and their revolvers were thrown into the river. After this slight delay the principals were able to get down to business. An onlooker described the protagonists:

'It did not take Morrissey long to peel. Throwing off his coat and white shirt, he stood in his red flannel undershirt, as brawny a young bruiser as the most enthusiastic admirer of muscle could desire to see. Poole had a powerful physique and carried himself the more gracefully of the two. Each stood over six feet and weighed close to two hundred pounds.' There was no ring but a space had been cleared on the cobbles. The fight began with some light sparring and then Morrissey made a bull-like rush at the other man. The experienced street-fighter ducked and seized Morrissey by the ankles. With enormous strength he threw Morrissey clear over his head and then leapt on his opponent as he lay breathless on the ground. They butted, clawed and pounded away at each other for two or three minutes, but Morrissey never recovered from his dreadful fall.

'I'm satisfied,' he gasped. 'I'm done.'

Morrissey had the greatest difficulty in escaping in one piece from the scene of combat, but his supporters managed to carry him through the jeering mob to the safety of the Bella Union saloon on Leonard Street, of which he was part-owner.

The fight was to be the start of some of the most dreadful disturbances ever witnessed on the streets of New York. Supporters of both men roamed the streets, fighting whenever they met.

On the evening of 24 February, Poole and a few cronies were drinking in a saloon when in walked Morrissey and some of his acolytes. At once Morrissey and Poole began to quarrel and had to be separated. Reluctantly, Morrissey and his men left the saloon.

Morrissey then went home to bed, but some of his companions returned to the saloon to settle things with Poole. One of them spat in Poole's face. Calmly the rough-and-tumble fighter took five $100 gold pieces from his pocket and said that he would bet that he could beat anyone in Morrissey's party in a fair fight.

There were no takers, but one of Morrissey's men, Jim Turner, who had recently been run out of San Francisco by the Vigilantes, drew a pistol and fired it at Poole. Turner managed only to shoot himself in the arm. One of the men present later described the situation:

'That was the signal for a general fusillade, and also for a general scamper. Unable to get out, those who had no stomach for the deadly sport took refuge behind counters and stools. One chap, George Deagle, actually walked into a pier mirror, supposing it in his terror to be an open door.' When the smoke and confusion finally cleared away, Bill Poole was lying mortally injured on the floor of the saloon. He survived for two weeks. On his death-bed he made a sworn statement to the effect that his shooting had been due to an organized plot by John Morrissey. With his last breath the rough-and-tumble champion of New York sighed, 'I die a true American!'

Morrissey and the men who had started the shooting in the saloon were indicted. The prize-fighter had so much political influence that there were three trials, the jury disagreeing at each one. In the end the prosecution abandoned the case and no one was punished for the shooting of Bill Poole.

# *All in a Day's Work*

London, December 1855

The prize-ring in 19th-century Britain owed its survival to those aristocratic patrons who were given the generic title of the Fancy. If these noblemen liked a fighter they would back him to the tune of thousands of pounds and reward their representative generously.

Gaining their support, however, was no easy matter. Jem Mace discovered this as a young bare-knuckle fighter trying to make his way in the world. In later years he was to win the world championship, become one of the game's greatest tutors, and continue sparring in his travelling booth well past his fiftieth birthday.

In his early days Mace was only too happy to be called to London to be given a trial before the members of the Rum-pus-pus club. This was an organization patronized by the wealthy and well-born who had an affinity with the ring. The club met every Wednesday in a room above the Cambrian Stores in St Martin's Lane. The members dined off roast beef, plum pudding and port at a table inside the ropes of a simulated boxing ring.

After dinner Jem Mace was brought into the room and introduced by the proprietor Nat Langham as a novice fresh from the country who hoped to earn the approval of the club's patrons. The diners withdrew from the ring and settled down to watch the youth display his fistic wares.

The first challenger was a member of the Rum-pus-pus

club, Lord Drumlanrig. Courteously the nobleman asked Mace to spar with him using the mufflers, as the sparring mittens were called.

Mace was in a quandary. He wanted to impress the influential members of the club but did not wish to hurt one of its best-known members. Drumlanrig settled the matter for him by attacking the young professional vigorously. Mace replied with spirit. In the space of a few rounds Drumlanrig's ruffled shirt was torn to ribbons and smothered in its owner's blood. Gracefully the peer gave Mace best and handed him a couple of sovereigns for his trouble.

The novice had passed his first test but much more was to be expected of him that evening. After Lord Drumlanrig had been assisted back to his seat by solicitous friends, the still bleeding challenger called out, 'Your novice is too good for me, Nat. Better set one of your pros at him!'

That was just what the proprietor had in mind. The next challenger to be wheeled out to test Mace was a veteran prize-fighter called Johnny Walker. Mace hammered the older man into submission after thirty brisk minutes. If he was hoping for a rest the young aspirant was to be disappointed. As he later recounted in his memoirs:

'Then they set a man called Mo Betson on to me, and when I had beaten him, yet another, whose name I forget, but whom I served likewise. That made four men I had defeated in one day.'

The patrons of the club approved of their new discovery and forecast a glowing future for the young fighter. To set him on his course they subscribed a purse of £5, in addition to the two sovereigns he had received for thrashing Lord Drumlanrig.

Mace's day was not yet over. He had impressed some of the younger swells so much that they hired him as an escort on their tour of London's nightlife that evening. It was Mace's task to ward off pickpockets and other low life as the young bloods visited the Coal Hole song and supper room, the Cyder Cellars, and other murky areas of the capital.

Mace was paid an additional guinea for acting as bodyguard. And to provide full value for money, in the course of the evening he also gave a display of muscle flexing and then borrowed a violin and played a jaunty solo for his patrons and their lady companions.

It was four o'clock in the morning before Jem Mace returned to Nat Langham's club to sleep. It was, he noted later, 'one of the most tiring, albeit enjoyable days I had spent in my life'.

# Fighting Ladies

## London, February, 1878

One of the strangest rivalries which existed in the boxing world in the 1870s was that between Selena Seaforth and Mademoiselle Daultry. Each lady claimed to be the champion woman boxer of the world and toured the halls hurling defiance and challenges at each other.

It all began when Abe Daltry, one time prize-fighter, professional sprinter and boxing instructor at the German Gymnasium in London, decided to enter show business and put together an act with his brother Joe and a lady called Selina Seaforth.

Daltry, who adopted the title of Professor as the result of his instructional duties at the German Gymnasium, taught Miss Seaforth the rudiments and renamed his brother Joe 'Corporal Higgins'.

Thus equipped, the trio embarked upon a music-hall career, being booked at a number of halls in London and the provinces. Their act consisted of low-comedy sketches, exhibitions of various types of self-defence and a display of boxing by Selina, who sparred with Abe and 'Corporal Higgins'.

At first the routine went well, as was evidenced by an advertisement placed in the *Referee* by Abe, extolling the virtues of the entertainment provided and including a favourable review from the provincial press.

21

*PROFESSOR ABE DALTRY*
and
Selina Seaforth
the talented Burlesque Actress and Vocalist
and champion Lady Pugilist
(something to hear and something to look at, not a dwarf)
assisted by Professor Higgins and Master Joshua
now starring and appearing with usual success,
Alhambra, Hull
*The Hull Daily News, 24 February*

Undoubtedly the most important feature in the
programme at this place this week is the entertainment
given by Professor Daltry and Miss Selina Seaforth. Miss
Seaforth is the champion female boxer of the world, and
her skill in the use of gloves is astonishing. She is
evidently well able to give a good account of herself in the
art of self-defence. This lady and the Professor are
assisted by Professor Higgins and Master Joshua.

Their Feats are received with warm approbation.

Unfortunately it was not long before the two brothers were
falling out. Joe claimed that he had devised most of the act and
that he deserved better billing and more money. Abe insisted
that he had played the major part in preparing the routines
and that he was in charge.

There was a stormy parting of the ways and Joe Daltry set
up his own act, complete with his own world champion female
boxer. To add insult to injury, he even gave her a slightly
altered version of the family name, calling her Mademoiselle
Daultry.

Abe Daltry was scandalized at the disloyalty and what he
regarded as the blatant poaching of ideas by his brother. The
two acts began to snipe at each other through the columns of
the sporting and music-hall press. After one such advertisement from Joe Daltry, his brother Abe responded in no
uncertain terms in the *Referee*:

*Note to Proprietors and Managers*

That party calling himself Corporal Higgins is using a
name Professor Abe Daltry gave him. Professor Abe
Daltry also taught Higgins what he knows. We have
never heard of the Royal Gymnasium, but we have heard
of the Broad Street Gymnasium, which was kept by
Professor Abe Daltry and was broken up.

It was not long before the incensed Abe Daltry was
addressing himself to the public again.

*Notice to Proprietors and Managers*

The person calling herself Champion Light-Weight
Boxer has never seen a boxing glove in her life. She has
only been on the stage five or six times, and she calls
herself a champion. She is more fit to weigh up tea and
sugar than to be a boxer. These new beginners want to
get their names up by challenging people. Wait until 'my
father-in-law puts me in a public house', then you can
challenge.

By this time Abe was getting a little incoherent as his
brother continued to prosper and issue challengs on behalf of
Mlle Daultry. A little later Abe had another blast in the
columns of the *Referee*

*Proprietors and Managers*
all know the talent of
Professor Daltry and Selina Seaforth.
The talent of new beginners has to be found out.
We don't know what Corporal Higgins means by
'drawing the peg', but we remember when he was nearly
'pegging out', and then we were the sufferers.
Manchester shortly, where we will explain all,
and that will put a stop to the P.O.O.

23

Throughout the controversy Joe Daltry and his companion seem to have been doing well, as was shown by the advertisement they inserted in the *Referee*:

The Original CORPORAL HIGGINS is now introducing an entirely New Sketch, entitled 'Fun in a Gymnasium', assisted by Mdlle Daultry, the Champion Lady Boxer, and Professor Finch, introducing their Refined Assault-at-Arms, consisting of Foils, Single-Sticks, Sword and Bayonet, Cavalry Sword, Exercise, Clubs, Wrestling, the Old English Game of Quarter-Staff, and Scientific Boxing. Higgins invites Proprietors and Managers to see the Show. Also a Lady Single Turn, Miss Alice Davidson, the Charming Ballad and Operatic Vocalist. Finish tonight Oxford, Middlesbrough. Monday next, Sheffield.

Both acts continued successfully on their way as they toured the country, with each lady claiming the championship. They never met in the ring, but as one contemporary writer noted, whenever business got slack, one of the Daltry brothers could be relied upon to drum up interest by challenging the female pugilist sponsored by the other.

# A Movable Fight

## Long Island, December 1887

When the middleweight champion Jack Dempsey defended his title against Johnny Regan it seemed for a time that the fight would never take place. The police kept such a close eye on both contestants that the first bout had to be postponed. On the second occasion thick fog made it impossible for the contest to be held.

Finally the match was made at Huntingdon on the north shore of Long Island. Unfortunately the organizers had forgotten to take the tide into account during their preparations. Matters were already bad enough because snow had been falling steadily ever since the bout began. But when, after eight rounds occupying eighteen minutes, the men found themselves ankle deep in the swirling water, a temporary halt was called.

The ring was struck while the fighters and many of the spectators were loaded on to a tug which nosed along the coast looking for a likely spot for the resumption of the contest.

After a sea journey of some twenty-five miles, a suitable location was found. The fighters, their seconds and the twenty-five or so remaining onlookers waded ashore, put the ropes up again and got the fight under way.

The two men fought fiercely for another thirty-seven rounds, lasting almost an hour, and Dempsey won by a knockout in forty-five rounds in locations twenty-five miles apart. The only consistent feature of the match was the snow, which continued to descend heavily throughout.

# The Great John L

## London, December 1887

John L Sullivan, the flamboyant and hard-living heavyweight champion of the world, sailed to Great Britain to investigate the possibility of meeting the British boxers Charlie Mitchell and Jem Smith. He stayed to tour the music-halls of Manchester, Newcastle, Derby, Glasgow, Dublin and a dozen other cities, rating headlines wherever he went. It was almost like being at home again.

Suddenly, though, enquiries began to be made about the champion behind the scenes. Someone appeared to be checking up on Sullivan, to ensure that his drinking habits were being kept in reasonable check on the tour.

The next step in the drama occurred on the evening of 8 December 1887. Sullivan had been the guest of honour at a dinner given by the Pelican Club. He was relaxing with a few friends after the meal when a young army officer approached the group. He handed Sullivan a note. The champion studied the contents and nodded.

'Tell them I won't disappoint them,' he told the officer.

With that brief sentence Sullivan committed himself to an appearance which was to hit the headlines of practically every newspaper in Europe and the USA. The message had been from the officers of the Scots Guards, inviting the champion to breakfast with them in their mess the following day. After breakfast, said the message, the officers would be pleased to take Mr Sullivan across to the Fencing Club, where he would be presented to His Royal Highness the Prince of Wales, who had expressed a desire to meet the champion of the world.

The next day Sullivan arrived as he had promised. With him were his manager and an American journalist named Arthur Brisbane. The gentlemen of the Guards regiment made every effort to make their guest feel at home and the meal was an elegant affair.

True to form, Sullivan was in no way abashed at being in such exalted company, which included officers from many crack regiments, among them Lord Randolph Churchill. The champion chatted pleasantly to everyone around him, eager to prove that he was no stranger to polite society.

Several hours later a hushed whisper reached Sullivan's hosts to the effect that the Prince of Wales had arrived at the Fencing Club. Sullivan was invited to cross the road to meet His Royal Highness. Expansively the champion agreed. In his present mellow mood he was ready to meet anyone, even his arch-rival Charlie Mitchell!

Sullivan and several of the senior officers crossed over to the Fencing Club. There was a moment's unpleasantness at the door when officials attempted to exclude Brisbane, the journalist. Sullivan vouched for the writer's discretion and the party was admitted. The newcomers were met by Sir Francis Knollys, equerry to the Prince.

'His Royal Highness desires very much to meet you, Sullivan,' he said. 'May I have the honour of presenting you?'

Sullivan nodded benevolently. 'You may!' he boomed. 'I reciprocate heartily the sentiments of the Prince.'

The encounter was a great success. Edward the Prince of Wales was a short, plump, bearded man of forty-six, languishing in the shadow of his formidable mother Queen Victoria. He was more than at home in theatrical and sporting circles. Sullivan was equally at ease.

'Next to Jem Smith,' he told the Prince, 'you're the man in England I most wanted to meet. How's your mother?'

While members of the Royal Household fluttered anxiously just out of earshot, the Prince and the prize-fighter sat and talked for an hour. Sullivan never disclosed the subjects of their conversation. It is believed that Edward discoursed on his visit to the USA and mentioned that both his sons were keen boxers.

The Prince had a further treat in store for himself. Presently the party moved into a large room in which a ring had been set up, to watch an exhibition of sparring between Jem Smith and Alf Greenfield. During the bout Sullivan excused himself and went to a dressing-room. Later he returned clad in emerald-green tights. He was followed by Jack Ashton, his permanent sparring partner, also stripped for action.

Before a delighted audience the two men fought a spirited four-round exhibition bout. When they had finished, the crowd, which included the Prince of Wales, nineteen earls and four colonels, applauded for almost five minutes.

Afterwards the Prince approached the sweating champion, shook him by the hand and wished him well during his stay in Britain. The crowd edged forward to hear Sullivan's last words to the Prince of Wales. The champion did not let them down.

'Goodbye,' he said heartily. 'Any time you're in Boston I want you to look me up. I'll see that you're treated right!'

# The Fight in the Rain

## Chantilly, March 1888

John L Sullivan, the American heavyweight champion of the world, always hated his perky and quick-witted British challenger, Charlie Mitchell.

They first met at Madison Square Garden in 1883. The much lighter Mitchell had caused a furore by flooring the world champion, but Sullivan had recovered to batter Mitchell into insensibility.

A year later they were matched to meet again. On the night of the bout Sullivan turned up at the arena rolling drunk and in no condition to fight. Lesser men would have slunk dismally away. Not so John L. He insisted on staggering down the aisle and making an incoherent speech from the ring to the 15,000 spectators, apologizing for being 'sick'. Such was the force of his personality and so firmly entrenched was his popularity, that he got away with it.

For ever afterwards Sullivan insisted that it was illness, not whisky, which had prevented him from keeping his engagement with Mitchell. In his ghosted autobiography, *Life and Reminiscences of a 19th Century Gladiator*, Sullivan passed off the incident by declaring, 'I grew careless in eating and drinking, and was thrown off my guard.'

It was to be another four years before the two men met again. This time they were matched under the London Prize Ring Rules for a bare-knuckle fight to the finish.

Negotiations for Mitchell were handled by his redoubtable

29

father-in-law, the notorious Pony Moore. Moore was a notorious 'sportsman'. An entertainer by profession – he ran a famous minstrel show – he was also a heavy gambler and a sharp businessman.

Moore saw to it that the ring measured twenty-four feet, which would suit the more elusive Mitchell, and that they would fight on turf, not boards, which should favour the smaller British fighter, who was lighter on his feet.

The venue selected was a field behind the stables on the estate of the Baron de Rothschild at Chantilly, not far from Paris. For three days before the contest, rain fell steadily, churning the turf into mud.

There were about seventy spectators, the usual motley collection of gentlemen, pickpockets, ex-pugs and journalists. The bout had not started when Billy Porter, a bank-robber on the run from the police in America, entered the ring, drew a revolver from either pocket of his overcoat, glared at the toughest of the British supporters and drawled, 'If anyone starts anything funny ... '

The rest of his words were drowned in a growl of fury from the crowd, but Porter had made his point and no one tried to interfere with the fight.

A flag decorated each corner. Sullivan's consisted of a spread-eagle and a shamrock, while Mitchell's bore his initials and, in rather larger letters, 'Backed by Pony Moore'.

The fighters appeared and a cheer went up. Sullivan strode over to his opponent and suggested a side-stake. He was waved aside by Pony Moore. At the sound of 'Time!' being called, Sullivan emerged like a galleon under sail, swinging his right hand.

'Come on, Charlie!' he jeered. 'Knock me down again!'

Mitchell was not to be drawn. As Sullivan came forward, he retreated. He retreated for six minutes before the champion finally caught up with him and knocked him down with a clubbing right. Mitchell grinned as his seconds helped him up. Mitchell always grinned.

Sullivan scored the second knockdown as well. He caught Mitchell in a corner again and floored him with a straight right. At this early stage in the contest Mitchell's seconds seemed in a worse state than their fighter. Pony Moore was groaning in agony, while Arthur Brisbane, straining his ears at the ringside, swore that another second was imploring Mitchell, 'Think of the kids, Charlie; the dear little kids at home, a-counting on you for bread!'

Mitchell went out and ran. For round after round he dodged, held and fell down. Sullivan ploughed doggedly through the mud after his elusive adversary, swinging his right hand like a scythe. The champion was growing increasingly exasperated.

'For God's sake, stand and fight!' he roared at one stage.

In the fifteenth round Mitchell made one of his rare sallies. He darted forward and hit Sullivan below the belt. A cry of 'Foul!' went up from the crowd, but Sullivan would have none of it.

'No foul! I don't win the fight that way!'

It was raining again now, but the fight went on. It lasted thirty-nine rounds and over three hours. The pace of the bout slowed to a crawl. Sullivan continued to lash out desperately, but Mitchell, his grin a blood-stained smear, danced just out of his opponent's reach.

Sullivan's wind had gone. Mitchell had been knocked down thirty-eight times but looked as if he could keep bobbing in slow motion well into the night.

'A draw! A draw!' chanted the bored spectators.

The two men fought on grimly, but the seed had been planted in their minds. To his dying day Sullivan claimed that he wanted to fight on. It is true that after the bout he sobbed in exhaustion. Yet someone, probably his chief second Jack Ashton, went over to Mitchell's corner and suggested they call the contest a draw.

Mitchell shrugged. 'We'll shake hands or fight on, just as John likes.'

Baldock, Mitchell's second, nodded quickly. Honour was satisfied. He took his man to the centre of the ring and muttered a few words to B J Angle, the referee, who beckoned to Sullivan. The exhausted champion lurched forward out of his corner, half-prepared to fight on. The referee ordered him to shake hands with Mitchell, and declared that the verdict was a draw.

At this point Sullivan began weeping and protesting bitterly. He begged for just a few more rounds, but it was all over. Spectators and participants alike began to head for their carriages.

Before they could reach the road, a squad of armed policemen surrounded the chief actors in the melodrama and arrested them. Prize-fighting was illegal in France, just as it was in England.

The rain continued to pour down as Sullivan trudged off to the nearest lock-up. The champion's teeth were chattering. He was frozen to the marrow, exhausted and depressed beyond endurance.

They put him in a cell next to Charlie Mitchell. The Briton took his arrest more philosophically than the aggrieved Sullivan. But then Mitchell had had more experience of being incarcerated.

The following morning Sullivan was released on a bail of £200. He promptly went on a monumental drinking bout. In the course of this he announced his intention of jumping bail. He was promptly rearrested and then released on a bail of £400.

He still jumped bail and returned to Britain. He had finished with Europe. He booked a passage back home. As he boarded the vessel he heard that the French authorities had fined him 2000 francs in his absence. He also heard that his total earnings on the five-month tour of Britain amounted to over $200,000.

Sullivan never fought in a bare-knuckle bout again. In future he was going to restrict himself to three-minute rounds with the gloves. He said as much in a public announcement.

'I want fighting,' he said simply. 'Not foot-racing!'

# *Lonsdale* vs. *John L?*

## New York, 1888

Hugh Lowther, fifth earl of Lonsdale, was a great patron of boxing and a much travelled man. He would sometimes write about his experiences, and once, in *The People*, gave an account of how he actually knocked out the great John L Sullivan in a private sparring contest behind closed doors at a riding academy near Central Park.

The peer gives a spirited account of the first rounds of their bout, and then goes on to describe how gradually he wore down and knocked out the champion of the world:

'Though I was certainly hard-pressed, I knew quite well that Sullivan was in a much worse plight. I had shaken him up time after time, and he was breathing hard, and finding it difficult to time his punches.

'As he came at me in the opening of the sixth, I decided it was now or never.

'I let fly with my right and caught him solid in the solar plexus, and he went down without a sound, apart from a faint grunt.

'He lay there for several minutes after the final count, and when I went over and put out my hand to shake his, his face wore a dazed sort of smile as he accepted my grip ... ' All very stirring stuff and a great triumph for the plucky amateur over the seasoned professional. There is only one drawback to the story. None of it ever happened!

Lonsdale was certainly in the USA in 1888, the year in

which he claimed the bout took place, but he never met John L Sullivan, in or out of the ring. For the first half of the year the champion was touring Britain, culminating in his bout in France with Charlie Mitchell. From June onwards he was very ill and in no condition to fight anyone.

Yet Lord Lonsdale told his story for the rest of his life and it was repeated in most of his obituaries when he died in 1941.

# The Pivot Punch

## San Francisco, August 1889

When George La Blanche, the Canadian who had served in the US Marines, heard that he was to meet the original Jack Dempsey, 'the Nonpareil', he was not particularly enthused at the prospect.

Not only was Dempsey an outstanding all-round boxer and fighter, he had already knocked La Blanche out in thirteen rounds in a contest for Dempsey's middleweight title.

The more La Blanche thought about it, the more he felt that he was on a hiding to nothing. Short of hitting the champion with a blackjack there seemed no way of beating him. The Canadian decided that he needed all the help he could get. For a start, he recruited Jimmy Carroll, an English lightweight, as his trainer.

Carroll was not a particularly good fighter but he was sneaky. La Blanche was well aware that he would require an extremely devious man in his corner to stand any chance against the champion.

Dutifully the challenger went into training under the watchful eye of his new handler. For weeks La Blanche ran and skipped and sparred. Carroll watched his every move. Nothing that he saw gave him the slightest hope that his man could defeat the mighty Dempsey.

'It'll take a miracle,' he muttered.

Miracles were in short supply in the run-up to the championship, but Carroll did have one desperate ploy. Jack

Dempsey was such a consummate boxer that he had an answer to every punch and combination that his opponent was likely to attempt. Suppose, however, that La Blanche could come up with a completely fresh punch? He would have just one chance because the intelligent champion would have worked out a counter if La Blanche tried it a second time. Carroll remembered a move from his street-fighting days.

'Have a go at this,' he ordered.

On the day of the fight Dempsey was in top form. He thrashed La Blanche for thirty-one consecutive rounds. The Canadian could do nothing against his much stronger and quicker opponent.

Again and again, between rounds, La Blanche begged Carroll to allow him to use the new move they had perfected at the training camp. Each time Carroll shook his head obdurately. La Blanche would have to wait until Dempsey was so confident that he would be expecting nothing from his opponent. After the thirty-first round the second finally nodded.

'The next round,' he muttered.

La Blanche staggered forward when the bell started the thirty-second round. Dempsey loomed up before him. The Canadian launched a left hook, as he had done a hundred times before. This time he deliberately missed and the blow sailed past Dempsey's head. In the same movement La Blanche pivoted on his heel and brought his arm back with tremendous force.

Some spectators said that he caught the champion on the jaw with his elbow, while others claimed that it was the back of his glove which caught Dempsey full in the mouth. Whichever it was, the force of the pivot blow was so dreadful that it robbed Dempsey of his senses. The champion fell unconscious on his face.

The referee counted the champion out while the crowd looked on in stunned silence. It was a blow never witnessed in the ring before. Everyone was sure it must have been illegal, but no one could be sure.

The pivot punch became the talk of boxing. La Blanche

36

claimed the victory and the title. He was granted neither. The pivot punch was banned and La Blanche's victory was ignored.

# Bad Day at Bruges

## Bruges, December 1889

Squire George Alexander Baird was an evil man. Drunken, profligate and immoral, he straddled the sporting world of the last decades of the 19th century like a poisonous spider.

He was an excellent amateur jockey who managed both to own the winner of the Derby and to be warned off the turf. Later he took an interest in prize-fighting and developed a retinue of boxers to go with his large string of horses.

Baird's interest in the ring began when he joined the notorious Pelican Club, a boisterous institution for young men about town with sporting interests. Among its members was Lord Lonsdale, one of the patrons of British boxing.

The pet of the Pelicans was the British heavyweight champion Jem Smith. Smith spanned the closing days of the bare-knuckle fighters and the opening era of the glove boxers. He was a sturdy, rather over-muscled man of great stamina but no outstanding skills as a fighter. He owed his reputation to two losing contests. One of these was with the gifted Irish-born American heavyweight Jake Kilrain. The bout lasted an incredible two-and-a-half hours and 106 rounds, in the course of which Smith was knocked down thirty-six times. The fight was declared a draw due to fading light, but even Smith admitted that his opponent had had the better of it.

Smith's second famous bout was with the West Indian heavyweight Peter Jackson. It was held at the Pelican Club and Smith was declared the loser on a disqualification after he had received a thrashing at the hands of his opponent.

Baird and many other members of the Pelican Club lost a great deal of money betting on Smith to beat Jackson. Immediately they set to work to find another adversary for Smith, in order to recoup their losses. Smith might not have been much of a champion but he was the best one they had.

The opponent selected for Jem Smith was a formidable Australian, Frank Slavin, the 'Sydney Cornstalk'. The two fighters were matched to meet on the tennis court of a retired British army officer in Bruges, the capital of West Flanders in Belgium.

Baird was determined not to lose money on this fight as he had when backing Smith to defeat Peter Jackson. He bet a large sum not that Smith would win but that the Englishman would not lose. That accomplished, the Squire set out to ensure that Slavin did not beat Jem Smith.

Accompanied by a large crowd of thugs armed with coshes and knuckledusters, Baird stood at the ringside in Bruges and watched grimly as Slavin and Smith embarked upon their bare-knuckle contest for £500 a side. The English champion put up a brave fight but as usual he was outclassed. Slavin hit him almost at will and it was obvious that it was only a matter of time before Smith conceded the bout.

Baird was not going to have that. As the fifteenth round approached its end, with Smith reeling helplessly, the Squire advanced on the ring with his motley crew of associates, shouting, 'Do in the Australian bastard!'

There were many other members of the Pelican Club present. Among them was Lord Mandeville. Together with a few fair-minded friends, Mandeville had been expecting trouble from Baird and was prepared for it. As the Squire advanced on the ring, Lord Mandeville reached for the belt around his waist and produced an enormous Bowie knife, which he brandished in the general direction of Baird and his thugs.

The heroic gang wavered and then turned and fled, with Squire Baird prominent in their ranks as they disappeared over the horizon.

However, the damage had been done. The referee, disgusted by what he had witnessed and fearing that Baird and his gang might regroup, declared in a loud voice, 'I refuse to act any longer. It is impossible for Slavin to get fair play. I will not stay and see him get killed. It is a draw!'

Smith had not lost to Slavin, so Baird and his cronies saved their money. Nevertheless, the Squire was expelled from the Pelican Club for his disgraceful conduct at Bruges. He died five years later at the age of thirty-two, having caught a chill at the ringside while watching a contest between Jim Hall and Bob Fitzsimmons in New Orleans.

# Moving Pictures

## Mexico, February 1896

In modern professional boxing, television rules. It is commonly agreed that a bout can be held in a garden shed and still make large profits for all concerned as long as the television rights are sold.

The relationship between moving pictures and professional boxing has not always been an easy one. The first filmed boxing match was produced by the inventor Thomas Edison in his New Jersey studio in 1894. Mike Leonard and Jack Cushing fought a six-round bout for the benefit of the cameras. Afterwards they were both arrested for taking part in an illegal prize-fight.

It did not take the shrewder professionals long to appreciate the financial opportunities offered by movie versions of their contests. Only two years after the Leonard–Cushing bout, the cameras were present at a major heavyweight bout between Bob Fitzsimmons and Peter Maher on the banks of the Rio Grande, on Mexican territory.

When the canny Fitzsimmons asked what his share of the movie rights was to be, he was told that these were the promoter's perquisites, not the fighters'. Enraged by this, Fitzsimmons promptly knocked Maher out in the first round, before the cameras could start rolling.

Even in those days the movie makers were a pragmatic lot. They later restaged the bout, with the two fighters simulating their efforts on the banks of the Rio Grande. This time both boxers were paid for their efforts.

# *Gun Law*

## San Francisco, December 1896

By the end of 1896, the British-born heavyweight Bob Fitzsimmons was very close to persuading James J Corbett to defend his world championship against him. While he was waiting for the champion to sign the contract, Fitzsimmons agreed to engage in an unimportant warm-up contest against the unskilled but enormously strong and durable ex-sailor Tom Sharkey.

Everyone expected Fitzsimmons to dispose of Sharkey in a round or two in their San Francisco bout, but in the event the contest turned out to be one of the greatest and most blatant frauds in ring history.

The purse offered was $10,000. When Sharkey's backers suggested that it should be allocated on a winner-take-all basis, instead of being alerted to the possibility of chicanery, Fitzsimmons agreed with alacrity.

Soon rumours began to spread that the fight was not going to be on the level. Originally Fitzsimmons had been a four-to-one favourite to win. As the day of the fight approached, the odds began to change in favour of Sharkey.

Then the name of the referee was announced. To the surprise of followers of the sport and the absolute consternation of Fitzsimmons's camp, it was declared that Wyatt Earp was to be the official in charge.

Earp was the notorious gun-fighter who had been deputy marshal of both Dodge City and Tombstone in the wildest days of the Wild West.

Martin Julian, Fitzsimmons's manager and brother-in-law, protested loudly, saying that he had it on good authority that a ring of San Francisco gamblers had backed Sharkey heavily and were doing their best to safeguard their wager, by any means at their disposal. Julian wanted to cancel the bout, but his fighter dissuaded him. Fitzsimmons pointed out that he was sure to knock Sharkey out, and that there was nothing a referee could do to prevent that. He was to learn to his cost that he was mistaken.

The bout took place before a capacity crowd of 15,000 people at the Mechanics' Pavilion. When Fitzsimmons and his handlers entered the ring they noticed that the reporters covering the fight had been removed from their customary ringside seats and placed in a gallery some distance away. This was an ominous sign.

When Wyatt Earp ducked under the ropes there was an angry roar from the spectators when they saw that the ex-marshal was wearing a six-shooter. The police captain in charge of public order in the stadium made him unbuckle his belt and hand the weapon over.

Earp then walked to the centre of the ring and made a short public statement. He admitted that there had been rumours that tonight's result had been fixed in advance, but he assured the spectators that he could be relied upon to be honest in all his doings, without fear or favour.

'I'll call things as I see them,' he promised grimly.

The bout started. For eight rounds it was all Fitzsimmons. Sharkey had nothing to offer but courage and strength. The ex-sailor was knocked down as early as the first round. In the eighth round Sharkey was reeling helplessly around the ring. Fitzsimmons moved in for the kill. He hit Sharkey with two stunning hooks to the jaw. The fighter collapsed in a heap and was counted out by the timekeeper.

Fitzsimmons turned to have his arm lifted in victory by the referee. Instead Earp ignored him and called the announcer into the ring. Curtly he announced that the English fighter had been disqualified for a low blow.

When this news was passed on to the spectators there was almost a riot. It was quelled when Earp reclaimed his six-shooter from the police captain at ringside. Grimly he buckled the belt around his waist and stared out at the crowd.

The noise died away at once. It did not resume until the former gun-fighter had left the arena. Then the uproar started again.

It was to no avail. The referee's decision was final, no matter how unfair it might have seemed. Sharkey, of course, declared that he had indeed been struck in the groin, but he refused to submit to a medical examination.

In a desperate effort to have the verdict reversed, Martin Julian arranged a court hearing in which he claimed that the promoters and Wyatt Earp had conspired to defraud his man of the decision.

Julian even produced one of Sharkey's sparring partners, who declared that he had heard Sharkey's handlers talking about the fixed fight, but it was wasted breath. The judge, plainly no lover of boxing, said that prize-fighting was illegal in California and that he could not care less if there had been any bias in Wyatt Earp's decision.

The result went on Bob Fitzsimmons's record as a loss by a disqualification. It was generally accepted that the Cornish-man had been cheated out of the decision. His championship bout went ahead.

# Ladies' Day

## Carson City, March 1897

When Bob Fitzsimmons, the lanky Cornishman with the devastating punch, challenged James J Corbett for the latter's heavyweight championship at Carson City, Nevada, there were more than twenty female spectators in a private box near the ringside, an unheard-of event in professional boxing circles.

One of these women was Fitzsimmons's wife Rose. She was to play a prominent part in the proceedings. A practical, down-to-earth woman, she watched with growing dismay as her husband assimilated a dreadful beating at the cultured fists of the champion. In the sixth round the English fighter was floored for a long count of nine.

Rose screamed at her husband to get up, assuring him that he could still beat Corbett. The dazed Fitzsimmons staggered to his feet but continued to ship heavy punishment.

Rose decided that her husband's chances would be improved if only he would switch his attack to the body. She passed on this information as loudly as she could.

'Hit him in the slats, Bob!' she yelled enthusiastically.

It may have been a coincidence, but in the thirteenth round the tired Fitzsimmons followed Rose's insistent advice and began to belabour Corbett about the ribs. Finally he pulled off a fistic surprise by knocking out the champion with a punch to the solar plexus.

When Corbett finally pulled himself to his feet he rushed

furiously over to the new champion's corner, demanding that the fight be resumed. Fitzsimmons gave him little satisfaction.

'I won't fight you,' he declared.

'You'll have to!' stormed the volatile Corbett. 'If you don't I'll tackle you in the street the next time I see you.'

'If you do that,' said Fitzsimmons, 'I'll kill you.'

That was an end to it. Fitzsimmons and his wife Rose set about cashing in on the championship by touring in a play that featured Fitzsimmons as a fighting blacksmith, once his trade. The first time he defended his title, he lost it.

# The Ringer

London, September 1898

Crosses and double-crosses were quite common in the boxing world at the end of the 19th century. A painful experience for one of the protagonists occurred when the British lightweight Dick Burge was matched with the black American Bobby Dobbs.

Dobbs was thirty at the time but still no slouch. His reputation was so fearsome that gamblers backing Burge approached the American camp with an offer of a considerable amount if the black fighter would lie down in the fifth round.

John Barnes, Dobbs's manager, had heard that such an approach was likely. For his meeting with the gamblers he took with him, instead of Dobbs, another black fighter, introducing the ringer as the American lightweight. Both boxers agreed to the deception and accepted the bribe.

Dobbs promptly went into serious training and put the money received from the gamblers on himself to win. In the meantime the other black fighter allowed himself to be seen in pubs and clubs, obviously out of condition.

On the day of the fight the gamblers demanded to see Dobbs for one last time. When the impersonator appeared, they produced knives and forced the ringer to swallow an extremely strong purgative which would weaken him for the contest.

The unfortunate stand-in spent the rest of the day occupied with the workings of his stomach. When the real Dobbs entered the ring, the gamblers saw that they had been duped. Burge had taken his training lightly, thinking that he would have nothing to beat. He received a severe thrashing and deliberately fouled his opponent in the eighth round, preferring to be disqualified rather than knocked out.

Barnes, Dobbs and the ringer sailed back to the USA, considerably richer as the result of their experiences.

# The Sunderland Riot

## Sunderland, August 1900

A number of enterprising boxers have attempted to cash in on their popularity by working up some sort of stage act. Back in the bare-knuckle days, Ben Caunt and the 7-feet-tall American Charles Freeman burlesqued a boxing match at the Lyceum and Olympic theatres. Another prize-fighter, Deaf Burke, would dress as a clown and entertain the crowd before his matches. This led to an engagement in the Christmas pantomime of *Valentine and Orson* in Manchester. Burke then announced that he was prepared to act in Shakespeare, particularly in some of the great Roman roles, but there were no takers.

By 1900, the music-hall boom in Great Britain and the popularity of vaudeville in the USA meant that stars like Marie Lloyd, Gus Chevalier and George Robey were earning £200 a week. Performers from all branches of the sporting and dramatic worlds clamoured for a share in these rewards.

Famous actors began to appear on the halls in dramatic sketches. That elegant actor Beerbohm Tree and his wife were once met in the wings by a pair of cheerful acrobats coming off-stage. They greeted the actor with enthusiasm.

''Ullo, 'Erbert. 'Ow are you then?'

The eminent thespian was worthy of the occasion. Bowing graciously, he replied:

'Very well, thank you. You know my wife Maud? Maud – the two Whacks. The two Whacks – Maud.'

Boxing champions were keen to display their acting talents upon the stage. James J Corbett, the former heavyweight champion, appeared in London in a dramatic sketch. One evening, the magnificently built ex-champion was talking in the street to the 4-feet-tall comedian Little Tich, when two ladies passed by.

'Look!' said one excitedly. 'There's Gentleman Jim Corbett!'

Her companion looked vaguely at the two men. 'Which one, dear?' she asked placidly.

One of the most popular of the bad acts starring sporting heroes was the road-show company production of *Uncle Tom's Cabin*, with the portly one-time heavyweight champion John L Sullivan playing the cruel overseer.

Sullivan was wickedly plagued on the tour by the ham actor who took the part of Uncle Tom, the noble slave. Not only did this actor consistently upstage the fuming former champion by wandering down to the footlights and declaiming at the audience; on one occasion he refused to leave the stage unless promised a rise.

Finally it all grew too much for the short-tempered John L. One evening, when the other actor had been particularly obstreperous, Sullivan approached a scene in which he was supposed to whip Uncle Tom by carrying on stage a genuine whip. He gave the actor a couple of sharp lashes, whereupon a free-for-all broke out on the stage. When the celebrated right hand of the champion swung into action, the performance was brought to a summary conclusion.

Most boxers who took to the halls confined their acts to exhibitions of boxing, ending with a challenge to any man in the audience to last three rounds with the fighter. One of these was the black American middleweight Frank Craig, the 'Harlem Coffee Cooler'.

Once, when appearing against John O'Brien at the National Sporting Club, members were intrigued to witness Craig dictating a telegram to one of the club's pages between rounds. When questioned, Craig replied that his landlady had promised to make him some apple dumplings for his supper.

Clearly O'Brien was not going to last too long against him, so the black fighter had wired his landlady to have the dumplings ready a little earlier than planned.

At Sunderland, however, Craig nearly met his come-uppance. He was appearing at the local music-hall, and after his sparring exhibition he issued the usual challenge to any man in the audience to last three rounds with him for a prize of £5.

The offer was taken up by a shipyard worker, a great local favourite. Craig knocked him flat in a few seconds. At the sight of the local champion on his back, the spectators rose in uproar. An orange, hurled with great force from the auditorium, struck Craig on the top of his shaven head, sending him to the floor to join his unconscious opponent.

Hundreds of the shipyard workers who were packing the gallery then advanced noisily on the stage, intent on vengeance. Craig staggered to his feet and managed to flee unsteadily to the haven of his dressing-room, just as the safety curtain was brought down on the stage.

The Sunderland riot, as it became known, went on for several hours. The police were called out to disperse the crowd surrounding the theatre. Later that night, a black acrobat who bore a superficial resemblance to Craig was set upon outside the music-hall and badly beaten by the mob.

# Boxing in the Dock

## London, June 1901

Towards the end of the 19th century, professional boxing in Great Britain was a squalid, hole-in-the-corner affair. The sport was dominated by gamblers and crooks, 'fixed' fights and unfair decisions were rife and spectators stood as much chance of being beaten up and robbed as they did of seeing a genuine boxing match.

The game was rescued to a great extent in 1891 when the National Sporting Club was formed. Its Covent Garden premises soon became the centre of British boxing. The highest of standards were maintained and an atmosphere of gentility and decorum was demanded among the guests.

Members, who included peers, high-ranking officers in the services, barristers and solicitors as well as wealthy business men, would dine in the club before adjourning to the auditorium, which seated about 1300. The matches presented were of the highest quality and scrupulously refereed. They were also conducted in absolute silence, for no partisan encouragement was permitted during the rounds.

In due course the NSC developed an international reputation for representing all that was best in boxing. It came, therefore, as something of a shock when, upon the anniversary of the club's first decade, its manager and some of its leading committee members found themselves appearing as defendants at London's Central Criminal Court, charged with manslaughter.

The case had been brought as the result of a contest at the club, held the previous April, between Jack Roberts and Billy Smith. Both men had previously appeared at the NSC against different opponents. Roberts was a Londoner while Smith, whose real name was Murray Livingstone, came from the USA. They had been matched over fifteen rounds, but Roberts, trailing on points, had rallied and knocked the American out in the seventh round. In his fall, Smith had hit his head against the floor of the ring. He had died soon afterwards in Charing Cross Hospital.

This fatality proved the last straw to the powerful anti-boxing lobby. Prize-fighting was already illegal in Great Britain but as the National Sporting Club was a private institution it had been allowed to conduct boxing matches as long as they were considered scientific exhibitions. Unfortunately, in the last four years there had been four deaths in the ring. On at least two previous occasions the NSC had avoided prosecution by the skin of its teeth. The authorities could no longer turn a blind eye.

Appearing in the dock with Jack Roberts were A F Bettinson, the surviving founder of the club; John Douglas, a wealthy timber merchant, who had refereed the bout; Eugene Corri, another referee, who had been the timekeeper; and the six seconds involved in the contest.

The case attracted enormous interest. In essence, boxing was on trial. Should the accused be found guilty of feloniously slaying Billy Smith, the NSC would probably close, and organized boxing in Great Britain would suffer a mortal blow.

One of the prosecuting counsel, R D Muir, made this point in his opening address. The purpose of the case, he said, was not so much to punish the defendants as to ensure that a halt was put to further exhibitions of boxing. If the bout carried out under the rules of the club was unlawful, then the defendants were criminally responsible for the death of the American boxer Smith. On the other hand, if it were proved to be a lawful contest in which death had accidentally ensued, then the defendants were not guilty. The case for the prosecution, Mr Muir argued, was that this had been a fight, not a scientific exhibition of the noble art of self-defence.

When John Douglas was questioned, he stressed his experience as a boxer, having won the amateur championship three years running, in 1875, 1876 and 1877. He agreed proudly that his son John, later to become an Olympic champion, was the current public schools boxing champion.

The defending counsel, Charles Gill, KC, asked Douglas to tell the court how he had prepared both contestants for their match in advance.

*Mr Gill*: Did you see them before the contest?

*Douglas*: I did. I had a conversation with them both and I cautioned them about boxing fairly, and doing anything that was underhand or anything of that sort, and the two men said, 'Oh, there is no fear about that, sir; we are the best of friends and only want to see who is the better boxer.' I said, 'All right, as long as you box fair it is all right, but if you do anything unfair I shall disqualify you without any further warning!'

Between them Gill and Douglas spent some time in trying to present a picture of the ill-fated contest as roughly the equivalent of a game of tennis at a vicarage tea-party.

*Mr Gill*: Would the hitting of men of this kind be very quick?

*Witness*: It was very quick in this case and very smart.

*Mr Gill*: One way in which they would show their skill would be in the guarding, slipping, ducking and getting away?

*Witness*: Yes, that is where Smith showed his skill in the one way, because he was so quick in avoiding Roberts.

Even the fatal eighth round was dismissed as having been an innocuous passage of arms in which no one seemed to be in any way distressed.

*Mr Gill*: At the beginning of the eighth round did Smith appear to be perfectly fresh?

*Witness*: They were practically the same as they were when they started the first round. There was no sign of weariness or distress to either man.

*Mr Gill*: Was there any reason why you should interfere?

*Witness*: No, because when the men went to their corners at the end of the seventh round, they were absolutely – to all appearances – the same. It looked as if something was the matter then; I thought Smith was pretending, as is often the case with American boxers. The round only lasted about twenty seconds, and before I could form a definite opinion, the man sank down on his knees and the thing was over.

A number of prominent members of the NSC were called to state that, properly conducted, boxing was an extremely safe sport, and that the officials of the National Sporting Club always took the greatest care over contests. Admiral the Hon Victor Montague stated that he had witnessed innumerable contests and competitions at the club, and could vouchsafe that they were conducted with the greatest precautions. The Earl of Kingston agreed entirely with the evidence of the witnesses as to the fairness with which the boxing was carried on, and the care exercised by the club officials.

Mr Gill had been representing most of the defendants in the trial. Jack Roberts, the accused boxer, had his own counsel. This was the famous Edward Marshall Hall, KC, briefed by Lord Lonsdale, a patron of the sport, on behalf of the boxer. At the outset the KC made his opinion of boxing clear. 'I happen to like and admire it myself as a sport which fosters and encourages the true spirit of Englishmen.'

Marshall Hall went on to pour scorn on those who would seek to alter the character of the sport. Facetiously he suggested:

'At all future boxing competitions, whether held at the National Sporting Club or anywhere else, the combatants should wear leather jerkins, under which bells should be concealed – electric, if possible. The boxing gloves should be of the largest size and should be plentifully smeared with chalk. For each chalk mark seen on an opponent's doublet the striker should be given a point. But if in the making of that mark he should happen to ring one of the bells, he should be instantly disqualified for unnecessary violence with the intention of effecting a knockout, and be liable to an indictment for manslaughter.'

Edward Marshall Hall ended his defence of the boxer on a more serious and reflective note:

'And for my client Roberts I will say this word, not because I feel that anything further needs to be urged on his behalf, but because I know that he deeply feels his position in which by a cruel accident he has been placed, and that this distress of his is not occasioned by thoughts in any way selfish. I will say this. If the deceased boxer Smith could only revisit these mundane scenes and see his three friends, who were also his seconds, charged with the manslaughter of himself he would be paralysed with horror and astonishment.'

In his summing up, the judge, Mr Justice Grantham, made no secret where his sympathies lay in the case. He took up the point made earlier by Edward Marshall Hall about the straightforward virtues of a true-blue Englishman electing to settle his differences with his fists.

'Now I cannot help saying that I am afraid, if my charges to juries were looked at, it would be found that I had on many occasions advised the people to use their fists ... instead of using the knife. If you have been jurymen here I daresay you have been witnesses to a great many trials, even in London, where unfortunate people have met their deaths from knives. At any rate, my experience in the North of England, in the large seaport towns, is, that I never go there without trying men who use knives.

'It is much better for a man to use the weapon that God has given him, namely his fists, because it is not so dangerous, and that is why it is that a great many people are fond of boxing. On the other hand, it is very desirable that proper boxing under proper rules should be kept up; all people should not be afraid of using their fists when necessary.'

The jury took only two minutes to consider their verdict.

*Clerk of the Court*: Do you find that the death was caused from a knockout blow?

*Foreman*: We do not, but that it was the result of an accident.

*Clerk*: Do you find that it was a fight or only a legitimate sparring contest?

*Foreman*: That it was a boxing contest.

*Clerk*: And you say that the defendants are Not Guilty?

*Foreman*: That is so.

The NSC had secured a significant victory. No one was still

entirely sure whether boxing was illegal or not, but the verdict in the Rex v Roberts and others case encouraged other promoters to stage matches and encourage the development of boxing in Great Britain.

# The Battle of Clayton Square

## Liverpool, November 1902

There have been a number of unsuccessful attempts to match boxers against wrestlers. Such bouts have usually had an over-rehearsed look to them, or else have been dreadfully dull.

Bob Fitzsimmons is said to have destroyed wrestling champion Ernest Roeber with a single blow in an incident at his training camp while he was preparing to challenge James J Corbett in 1897, but this may well have been a press agent's fantasy. A few years later, wrestler Farmer Burns was reported to have pinned former middleweight boxing champion Billy Papke in eighteen seconds in a match for $1000 a side, after Papke had jeered at the wrestler.

Jack Dempsey certainly had a series of knockout victories over wrestlers in the 1940s. The one-time world heavyweight champion had been picking up a little loose change refereeing wrestling matches. The tank-town tour had not been going too well, so it was decided to beef it up by having Dempsey fall foul of the various 'villains' in the bouts he was refereeing. Dempsey would promptly challenge the wrestler to a bout with the gloves and then knock him out in some dreary tent show.

Even the great Muhammad Ali once took on a wrestler. In Tokyo in 1976, he fought a grappler called Antonio Inoki. At the beginning of the match Inoki dived to the canvas and spent the entire bout kicking up at Ali's legs in a dismal spectacle.

However, there was one occasion when boxers fought

wrestlers in a contest which was both exciting and genuine. It took place in Liverpool in 1902, and became known as the Battle of Clayton Square.

The instigator of the brawl was a brash young impresario named C B Cochran. Cochran had teamed up with a Russian wrestler called Georges Hackenschmidt. Wrestling was very popular in Lancashire, so Cochran took a three-month lease on the derelict Prince of Wales theatre in Clayton Square. He announced that Hackenschmidt and other wrestlers would be fighting on-stage.

The owner of the theatre was horrified when he discovered the purpose for which Cochran intended it. Wrestling was regarded as a squalid sport, and he feared he might lose his licence. He forbade Cochran to use his theatre to stage wrestling matches.

Cheerfully, Cochran ignored the ban, sending out hundreds of men with sandwich-boards advertising the forthcoming bouts. The distracted owner sent out hundreds more men with display boards announcing that the wrestling certainly would not take place. Feelings were soon at fever pitch. Rival board carriers fought when they met in the streets.

Cochran then announced that the main event on the first night would be a special bout between Georges Hacken-schmidt and a local wrestler, former British champion Tom Cannon. In fact Cannon, exhausted and impoverished, had recently retired and was back working in the pits he had left twenty years previously, but the gullible public accepted the bout as a great event.

On the opening night the theatre was besieged by would-be patrons clamouring for tickets. For weeks beforehand Hackenschmidt and the other wrestlers had been guarding the place to prevent the owner trying to resume possession. Now it looked as if Cochran had triumphed.

The resourceful owner was not yet beaten. Just as the spectators were beginning to pour into the theatre, all the lights went out. The gas pipes had been cut. Lesser men might have given up, but not C B Cochran. He sent men out to scour the city for gas fitters. Meanwhile he delivered an impassioned address to the mob in the square outside the theatre, promising them that the fight would go on if only they were patient.

Enough fitters were rounded up. Cochran secured the loyalty of the leading technician by promising him that he could be the timekeeper for the main event. The pipes were repaired, the lights fluttered on and the show began.

The opening night was a great success. Hackenschmidt had little trouble in disposing of the veteran Cannon, but the Russian's impressive strength and physique awed the audience. The supporting bouts were colourful enough to ensure packed houses for the entire three-month run.

Then the owner, who surely deserved some prize for perseverance, struck again. He found a clause in the small print of the contract which stated that the lessee had to be out of the theatre by midnight after every performance, and demanded that the local police should enforce it. After the show on the second night, the wrestlers were escorted from the building by the Liverpool constabulary. As soon as Cochran, protesting vigorously, had also been ejected, the owner moved in with a dozen of the toughest prize-fighters he had been able to recruit in the whole of Lancashire. These were men convinced that they would have no trouble with a group of ponderous wrestlers.

The following morning a determined Cochran led his wrestlers into Clayton Square. They discovered that the doors and windows were barred and that the owner and his boxers were in possession of the theatre.

Cochran withdrew with his men to a corner of Clayton Square and subjected his followers to a brief harangue. Then they turned and stormed the building.

It was quite a battle. After a desperate struggle, the wrestlers managed to wrench one of the doors off its hinges, and rushed into the theatre. They lumbered up a narrow flight of stairs only to be turned back by one of the prize-fighters wielding a fire-hose. Three times the wrestlers scrambled up the stairs, and three times the concentrated jet of water drove them back.

At the fourth attempt Hackenschmidt and his companions managed to reach the top of the stairs, bruised and soaked. The fighter who had been directing the hose on them lost his nerve and turned to flee. He was too late. Ten enormous professional wrestlers were upon him. History does not reveal the fate of the hapless wielder of the hose.

Throughout the battle for possession of the stairs, Cochran had been urging on his men with great vehemence. In his excitement he lost contact with the main body of wrestlers and found himself charging alone into the theatre. He reached the top of another flight of stairs and turned a corner to find six or seven of the owner's prize-fighters waiting for him.

They descended on the promoter in a concerted rush and hurled him bodily down the stairs into the street. By some miracle the irrepressible Cochran was not seriously injured. He staggered to his feet and lurched back into the theatre.

By this time the main fight was almost over. Only a few desperate minor skirmishes were still going on. Outside a roped square the prize-fighters had proved no match for the enraged wrestlers. Once more C B Cochran was in possession of the Prince of Wales Theatre.

It proved a Pyrrhic victory. The owner had not been idle overnight. Not only had the gas pipes been cut again but all the seats had been removed from the theatre as well. There would be no more wrestling in the Liverpool theatre.

Nevertheless, the publicity had been invaluable. Other cities clamoured to see the participants of the Battle of Clayton Square in which the wrestlers had humiliated the boxers. Cochran secured for Hackenschmidt an engagement in Manchester at £150 a week. Within twelve months the Russian Lion was famous all over Britain. Wrestling had become the latest rage and C B Cochran was launched upon his career as an impresario.

# The New Division

## Detroit, April 1903

Boxing managers are a much maligned breed. They are accused of being heartless exploiters who take 25 per cent of the purse and none of the punches. Heavyweight Buster Mathis summed up the feelings of many fighters when he said, 'The only thing I know about managers is that when the bell sounds, I go one way into the middle of the ring and they go the other way out of it!'

However, a number of handlers have more than earned their cut of a fighter's earnings. One of these was the Chicago manager Lou Houseman, who was also a boxing writer for the *Inter-Ocean*.

Houseman's chief fighter was a more than useful middleweight called Jack Root. Unfortunately, Root began to put on weight until he reached the 12-stone mark. This was too heavy for the middleweight division but not nearly big enough to allow Root to fight 15-stone heavyweights with any chance of success.

Lou Houseman was an ingenious fellow. If his fighter did not fit the weight divisions, then he would make a weight division fit his fighter. Through his column in the Chicago *Inter-Ocean* the manager began campaigning for the introduction of a new weight division between the middle and heavyweight classes. Houseman suggested that this new class be called the light heavyweight championship.

Other sports writers began to take the matter up. Once he

had got the ball rolling, Houseman went to work. He promptly staged the first contest for the light heavyweight championship of the world. Not altogether surprisingly, one of the contestants was his own fighter Jack Root.

The other contender had once been a big name but was now rather past it in fighting terms. He was Norman Selby, better known as Kid McCoy. McCoy was a brilliant boxer and an extremely shrewd operator who had sailed close to the wind on a number of occasions. One of his bouts, with James J Corbett, had been such a blatant 'fix' that it led to boxing being banned in New York for some time.

McCoy was not above trading in on the drawing power of his name. More than once he had booked himself to appear in several locations on the same evening, overcoming the logistical problem by sending a ringer, claiming to be Kid McCoy, to one of the matches. Promoters had grown wise to this ploy and had insisted on the Kid being less generous with his doppelgängers. To reinforce this point they had taken to billing the boxer as 'the real McCoy', a phrase which later entered the lexicon.

McCoy could not match the speed and punching power of his opponent and after ten rounds Root was declared the first light heavyweight champion of the world.

Lou Houseman had established a precedent which was to last until the 1980s, when the World Boxing Association stripped Sean O'Grady of his lightweight title for not defending it on time. Completely unperturbed, Sean's manager and father, Pat, promptly formed his own boxing body, the World Athletic Association, and declared his son the undisputed champion again.

# Cuffs and Kicks

## London, May 1906

Pedlar Palmer was known as the 'Box of Tricks', so effective was the little bantamweight's fighting style. He won the British title by defeating Billy Plimmer but was knocked out in a single round when he fought the American Terry McGovern for the world title.

A perky character, given to gambling and apt to get into more than his share of trouble outside the ring, Palmer was usually ready to have a go at any opponent within the roped square.

One of his most unusual contests took place at the Britannia Theatre in Hoxton. Palmer had been matched with the French champion, Louis Anastasie, at La Boxe Savante, a form of fighting popular in France in which boxing gloves were worn but participants were also allowed to kick. It had been agreed that for the duration of the bout Palmer would stick to the orthodox boxing style, using only his gloved fists, but that Anastasie could use both fists and feet.

The first round saw Palmer on top as he hustled the Frenchman around the ring, not giving him a chance to get set to deliver a kick. By the second round Anastasie had got the hang of Palmer's rushing tactics. The Frenchman danced around the edge of the ring, delivering graceful but extremely hard kicks to all portions of the British fighter's anatomy. This time it was Palmer who was dazed at the bell.

In the third round it was all Anastasie again. He peppered

the tiny Englishman with well-placed kicks, sending the Englishman reeling again and again.

Finally Palmer could take no more. Ignoring the stipulations of the bout, he decided that a suitable motto for the occasion would be 'When in Rome ...' He took one particularly hard kick to the head, swore viciously and dashed at Anastasie. The Frenchman smiled, anticipating another misplaced flurry of punches. Instead Palmer skidded to a halt and with great deliberation kicked his opponent in the groin.

Pedlar Palmer was disqualified.

# A Trusting Man

## London, December 1907

Tommy Burns, the Canadian, was the smallest man to win the world heavyweight title. He was also one of the shrewdest. When he came to Great Britain without a manager in 1910, a number of promoters thought that they were on to a good thing. They were in for a nasty surprise.

The first institution to feel the impact of Burns's negotiating skills was the National Sporting Club, the dignified headquarters of British boxing. The NSC was more accustomed to fighters who touched their forelocks and remained outside on the doormat until they were called in to display their wares. It was not like that with Tommy Burns. He agreed to fight the British champion, the pedestrian Gunner Moir, but demanded an unprecedented £3000 for his title defence.

Reluctantly the committee agreed, but their troubles were only beginning. On the night of the fight, when Burns entered the ring, he demanded in a loud voice that the entire sum be handed over to him before the contest began.

There were expostulations and recriminations, but the champion was adamant. No fee, no fight. With the greatest reluctance the club manager handed over the notes. Burns gave them to the referee to hold for him, and proceeded to knock Gunner Moir out in ten one-sided rounds.

Later, Burns gave a rather unconvincing explanation for his actions at the NSC:

'These are the facts,' he wrote. 'The first thing I was told when I landed in England was that you had a law whereby a man need not pay a bet if he didn't want to ... I had my own money at stake, and, naturally, I didn't want to risk it for nothing. So I mentioned what I had been told to the officials of the National Sporting Club, and it was suggested, more, I think, with a view to being friendly than for any other reason, that if both the side-bets were handed to the referee before the fight, to be given to the winner at its conclusion ... there could be no possibility of trouble. Naturally, I had no objection to make to this, and, equally naturally, as I think, I just enquired whether this had been done when I got into the ring.'

It was an ingenuous response, which ignored the fact that Burns had demanded his purse, not his bets, but by this time he was locked in combat with another management, the promoters of Wonderland in the East End of London.

In February 1911, Burns agreed to fight Jack Palmer, the former British champion, for 50 per cent of the take. The promoters, Harry Jacobs and Harry Woolfe, rubbed their hands with glee at the prospect of milking the champion as hard as they could.

Their anticipation waned when, the night before the contest, Burns arrived with a set of padlocks and changed every one in the arena, so that only the front door remained open. On the night of the bout he sat in the box office, counted every spectator admitted and then totted up the receipts, taking his half-share away with him in a bag. Only then did he change into his ring kit and, almost as an afterthought, knock Jack Palmer out in the fourth round.

Burns might have remained longer in Britain, to the chagrin of the country's boxing promoters, but he left hurriedly when he heard that his challenger, the mighty Jack Johnson, was hard on his heels. Burns was not afraid to meet the terrifying negro but someone was going to have to pay him £6000 for the privilege. No British promoter could countenance letting this amount of money go, so Burns sailed for Australia, where the showman Hugh McIntosh was only too pleased to stage the championship, and make a hearty profit out of Burns's losing effort.

# The Extra Round

## London, July 1908

The 1908 Olympics, held in London as an adjunct to the Franco-British Trade Exhibition, came as close to being a shambles as any large international sporting event could be. Just about everything that could go wrong did. Had it not been for the final of the middleweight boxing competition the whole tournament might have been regarded as a non-event.

The opening ceremony was performed by King Edward VII at the newly constructed White City Stadium at Shepherds Bush, housing 70,000 spectators.

The complaints and objections started almost at once. Sweden and the USA discovered that their flags were not flying above the stadium. Russia insisted that the Finns parade under the Russian banner or not at all. The Irish complained bitterly at being included in the British team. The Americans objected to the presence in the Canadian team of a Red Indian called Tom Longboat, insisting that he was a professional runner.

Canada and France protested about dubious decisions in the cycle racing, and the Swedish wrestlers walked out of the Greco-Roman competition. In one of the first finals, a City of London policeman called James Barrett was considered to have a good chance of winning. At a crucial moment one of his American rivals managed to drop the shot on Barrett's ankle, putting him out of the event.

The tug-of-war final was scheduled between the City of

Liverpool police and the American team. The Americans objected that the police were wearing boots. The policemen replied coldly that they always did and refused to meet the objection by removing them. The Americans attempted one pull against the beefy policemen, lost it and retired in a huff.

In the final of the 400 metres there were three Americans and a lone Briton. The Americans were adjudged to have impeded the progress of the British runner, Lieutenant Wyndham Halswell, and the event was declared 'no race' and ordered to be rerun. The Americans argued that they had done nothing wrong and refused to take part in the second race. Halswell ran the final on his own.

Off the track the boxing events proceeded with less fuss. That year Britain won all the gold medals, mainly because there were many more British entrants than from any other nation.

One bout was declared to have been the finest amateur contest ever seen in Great Britain. It was the middleweight final between the British representative J W H T Douglas and his Australian rival Reginald 'Snowy' Baker.

Douglas was one of the great all-rounders of his day. At the time of the Olympics he had represented England at football and was in the Essex cricket side. Later he was to go on to captain England and help win the Ashes.

His bout with Baker was a classic, with neither man giving an inch. So close was their encounter that at the end of the three rounds neither the referee nor the judges were able to separate the two contestants. So undecided were they that the boxers were ordered to fight an extra round! They did so and Douglas scraped home on points.

Baker became one of his country's best-known amateur boxers, winning titles at four different weights in the Australian championships.

Douglas served with distinction in the First World War and became an autocratic referee at the National Sporting Club, while working in the timber business. He was very close to his father, who was president of the Essex cricket club and owned the mortgage on the county ground.

J W H T Douglas died in 1930 while trying to save his father in an accident at sea. The vessel upon which they were returning from a holiday in Norway, the SS *Oberon*, was in collision with another boat off the coast of Denmark. Douglas's father went over the side and the athlete dived after him. Both men were drowned.

During his cricket career, Douglas was known as 'Johnny Won't Hit Today' for his initials and defensive style. He retained his interest in boxing until the end. While on a tour of Australia with the England team, he was the guest of honour at a civic reception. He replied to the speech of welcome by saying simply:

'Mr Mayor and Gentlemen, I can't make a speech beyond saying thank you, but I'm ready to box any man in the room three rounds!'

# The Sporting Spirit

## Los Angeles, September 1908

Stanley Ketchel was the original hustler. When he was middleweight champion of the world he would still enter mining saloons dressed as a bum and challenge the biggest man in the place to a fight for five bucks a side.

A little later he decided to cash in on his title by emulating world heavyweight champion John L Sullivan. The Boston Strong Boy had made a great deal of money by touring the Mid-West challenging any man to stand up to him for a few rounds and thus earn $100.

This seemed like money for old rope to Ketchel, so he embarked on his own tour of the theatres, challenging any man to last three rounds with him. Unfortunately, quite a few did. Ketchel was capable of knocking out any amateur, but he only weighed a little over 11 stone and some of the miners and cowboys he encountered were fifty pounds heavier than he was and managed to last to the final bell.

This was costing the champion money and was not to be encouraged. Accordingly Ketchel set out to remedy the situation. He continued to pitch his makeshift ring on the theatre stages, but he stationed an accomplice behind the curtain at the back of the stage. If a challenger looked like giving Ketchel any trouble, the middleweight champion would manoeuvre the other man until his back was to the curtain. Ketchel's friend would peer through a slit in the material and bring down a cosh on the head of the unsuspecting challenger.

Presumably Ketchel hoped that the pole-axed victim would conclude he had been struck by a punch too swift and deadly to be spotted by the naked eye. In any event, the champion no longer had to face the embarrassment of paying out $100 to any of the hopefuls facing him.

Given this talent for larceny, it came as a considerable surprise when Stanley Ketchel was himself outsmarted and deprived of his title by a piece of blatant cheating.

It happened when Ketchel fought Billy Papke, a man he had already defeated earlier that year. The champion expected no trouble from his opponent and when the bout started he walked across the ring, hand extended for the usual pre-match handshake. Papke had been expecting this. Instead of touching gloves he drove his left with all his force into the champion's face. Ketchel staggered back and Papke crossed his right, closing both of Ketchel's eyes with a single punch to the bridge of the nose.

Ketchel fought back on instinct alone but took a dreadful beating for twelve rounds before being knocked out. They fought again in San Francisco. This time there was no attempt to shake hands before the bout. Ketchel was on top from the start, but purposely did not knock Papke out until he had punished his opponent severely. He did not finish the bout until the eleventh round.

Afterwards Ketchel spoke to the newspapers: 'I anticipated the result long before I entered the ring and backed myself with my own money. Papke's last victory was an accident. Under proper conditions I am willing to fight him again.'

They did fight again and Ketchel won over twenty rounds, but time was running out for the champion. In the following year, 1910, he was murdered, shot in the back by the farmhand boyfriend of a girl to whom Ketchel had made advances.

# The Third Man

## New York, October 1910

Abe Attell, the featherweight champion of the world, had been around a long time. He started boxing in 1910. A decade later when he met Eddie Kelly in a small hall on the outskirts of New York, he had engaged in more than 150 contests.

Kelly, a good journeyman boxer, was almost as experienced. The two had met three times before, in New Orleans, Savannah and Seattle, with the champion winning on each occasion.

Before their bout in New York the two veterans decided to put on a good show for the patrons, but not to hit each other too hard. At a time when boxers had fifteen to twenty bouts a year, this was a fairly common arrangement in unimportant bouts.

Unfortunately for the fighters, the referee turned out to be both young and enthusiastic. For a round he watched the stick-and-move tactics of the contestants with a jaundiced eye. At the start of the second round he called the two men to the centre of the ring and in a loud voice admonished them and demanded more action.

Attell and Kelly were scandalized at being thus addressed. They were accustomed to more respect from the third man in the ring. Both fighters decided to treat the referee's curt remarks as a momentary aberration, probably made in the heat of the moment. They continued with their stately pavan. Again the referee stopped them and called for more effort.

This went on for another couple of rounds. To the consternation of the fighters, the crowd began to side with the referee. Plainly this was a state of affairs no self-respecting pros could tolerate. The two men went into a clinch.

'When he says "Break!" jump back,' whispered the champion.

The referee called upon the two men to step back. Obediently Kelly jumped out of the way. At the same second Attell smashed over his right and 'accidentally' caught the unsuspecting referee on the jaw, sending him tumbling to the canvas.

The third man may have been green, but he had style. Clutching his jaw, he scrambled to his feet and glared at the champion.

'That's better, Attell,' he rasped. He pointed at the innocent-looking Kelly. 'Only next time do it to him!'

Attell knocked Eddie Kelly out in the fourth round.

# The Double Knockout

During the opening decades of the 20th century, a number of boxing matches came under suspicion of being rigged. Controlling bodies, where they existed at all, were weak and ineffectual. Gamblers controlled the game and there were always fighters and referees who could be bribed or threatened.

Sometimes, however, things went wrong and, in a despairing effort to keep to the script, drama was sometimes turned into high farce.

When Ad Wolgast defended his world lightweight title against Indian Joe Rivers in 1912, it was the first time that he had put his championship on the line. Wolgast was an all-action brawler, while Rivers was reputed to be more of a scientific boxer who would put up a good enough show but was unlikely to give the champion too much trouble.

Known as the 'Michigan Wildcat', Wolgast was an acerbic character with scant regard for the quality of his opponents and contemptuous of their shortcomings. When he fought Knockout Brown in Philadelphia, he discovered that his southpaw opponent in this 1911 contest was cross-eyed. Wolgast loudly requested his adversary to hit where he was looking.

Joe Rivers had genuine Indian blood in his veins. He had spent most of his brief career fighting as a featherweight. To step up a weight against such a dynamic performer as Wolgast

75

was considered by most followers of boxing as asking for trouble.

To be on the safe side, Wolgast's handlers insisted on the champion's prerogative of naming the referee. In this case it was Jack Welch, a docile 'house' official who would do as the promoter demanded.

The bout was held before 11,000 spectators in an open-air stadium. To the surprise of the majority of the crowd Rivers, although only nineteen, started off by taking the fight to the champion, pumping a deadly left hand into Wolgast's face again and again.

For the first four rounds it looked as if the challenger might be going to cause an upset. Then Wolgast began to call on his years of experience. The champion did everything he could to slow his adversary down, clutching him in the clinches and pushing and pulling him across the ring. At the same time he bombarded his younger opponent's ears with a monotonous, non-stop flow of obscenities and insults, hoping to jolt Rivers out of his calm.

By the end of the twelfth round Wolgast realized that his tactics were not working. Rivers, although battered and tired, was still fighting back strongly. For his part the out-of-condition Wolgast could hardly lift his weary arms. He told his seconds that he had had enough and demanded they throw in the towel.

There was far too much money riding on the result to allow this. One of his seconds threatened to crown the champion with his own water bottle unless he went out to face Rivers again. At the same time he reminded the fighter that they had an ace-in-the-hole in the portly shape of the referee. Reluctantly Wolgast shuffled out to start the thirteenth round.

Referee Jack Welch realized that something above and beyond the call of duty was expected of him if he was to safeguard the thousands of dollars riding on a victory for the champion. He did not have the faintest idea how he was to accomplish this. But Welch was a pragmatist. Something would turn up.

It did. Summoning up all his remaining strength, Wolgast

staggered across the ring and hit Rivers full in the groin. At the same moment, Rivers, seeing the champion's unprotected jaw, crossed his own right, landing it on the button.

Both punches hit home simultaneously. Rivers crumpled and fell writhing to the ground. Wolgast tumbled senseless on top of him. The spectators screamed for a foul, demanding that Welch disqualify the champion.

Jack Welch goggled at the prostrate boxers. Hesitantly he started to count. Neither fighter moved. Then Welch had an idea. He reached down and, without missing a beat in his count, scooped Ad Wolgast off the floor, supporting the unconscious champion tenderly as he counted out the paralysed Joe Rivers.

At the stroke of 'ten', Jack Welch shifted his grip and lifted the hand of the oblivious Wolgast in a token of the champion's victory. His duty done, Welch then dropped Wolgast back to the canvas and dived through the ropes to make his escape before most of the spectators could believe the evidence of their own eyes.

A doctor confirmed that Joe Rivers had been badly fouled, but the referee's verdict could not be reversed, especially as Jack Welch had prudently gone into hiding. When he emerged, almost a month later, Welch claimed that as Wolgast had landed on top of Rivers, the challenger had obviously been knocked out first and that therefore Rivers had been counted out a fraction of a second before his opponent. He had held the champion up, declared Welch plaintively, to make that point plain.

There were many protests from Rivers's camp, but the unfortunate Indian Joe never got another shot at the title. Wolgast fought a few nondescript exhibition bouts and several no-decision contests, and later that same year he defended his title against Willie Ritchie.

After the scandal of the Indian Joe Rivers fiasco, there was no way that Jack Welch was going to be employed again as third man in the ring. Wolgast had to make do with an honest official, Jim Griffin. The champion still tried his own special methods of bending the rules and was disqualified in the sixteenth round.

Four years later, in 1916, Wolgast managed to persuade the

current lightweight champion, Freddy Welsh of Wales, to defend his title against him in Denver. Wolgast lost again – on a foul in the eleventh round.

In 1920, Wolgast's career came to an end. He had taken too many punches and could remember nothing of his long ring career. He was sent to a sanitorium for the mentally ill in Camarillo, California.

Wolgast was to spend the rest of his life there, until his death thirty-eight years later, in 1958. For his entire period in the sanitorium Wolgast thought that he was in training for some championship fight. He worked out every day in order to be ready for his big chance, when it came.

# The Café de Champion

## Las Vegas, July 1912

Jack Johnson, the heavyweight champion of the world, fought only once in 1912, the fourth year of his reign. Even so, it was not a dull year for the black heavyweight.

The solitary bout was against the rather shop-soiled veteran Fireman Jim Flynn. Flynn promised that he would die in his attempt to win the title. If he lost, he declared, he would order the promoter to shoot him.

In fact the challenger knew that he had little chance of winning a fair fight. That did not worry him, as he had already decided to fight a foul one. More specifically, he planned to butt Johnson with the top of his bullet head at every opportunity.

Flynn's intention of using dirty tactics became so apparent during training sessions that his trainer resigned in disgust.

The fight turned out to be a financial failure, with only a small crowd bothering to turn up. From the beginning Johnson had the bout well in hand, punishing Flynn severely.

Flynn did his best to put his plan into action. Again and again he leapt off the ground with both feet, trying to smash his skull into Johnson's face. He succeeded only in enraging the referee. The champion ignored Flynn's attempts to foul him and continued to pound his opponent into submission.

In the ninth round the bout was stopped in Johnson's favour, not by the referee but by the local police, disgusted by the bleeding and bruised state of Flynn.

79

It was the last good thing that happened to Johnson in 1912. He was already under indictment for attempting to smuggle a diamond necklace into the country. That was just the start.

Immediately after the Jim Flynn fight the champion opened a Chicago bar which he called the Café de Champion. Soon afterwards his wife Etta committed suicide. The newspapers, who believed that a black man should know his place, claimed that Etta, a white woman, had shot herself because she could not cope with her husband's flamboyant love affairs.

Less than a month later Johnson and his already notorious bar were in the headlines again. This time it was the champion who had been shot. The culprit was one of the coloured singers at the Café de Champion, Adah Banks. She had resented the attention Johnson had been paying to Lucille Cameron, a white secretary at the bar, and had fired a bullet into the heavyweight's foot.

It transpired that Lucille had run away from home. Her romance with Johnson was reported in all the newspapers. At this stage Lucille's mother, Mrs Cameron-Falconet, entered the action. She employed a legal eagle, Charlie Erbstein, to threaten Jack Johnson. Charlie did so with gusto, engaging the champion in a spirited altercation at the Café de Champion, beneath a celebrated portrait of Johnson framed in diamonds.

Mrs Cameron-Falconet then claimed that the black title-holder was exercising an evil hypnotic influence over her young daughter. The gullible authorities arrested Lucille and kept her in an hotel room where, they claimed, she would be immune to Johnson's supernatural powers.

The country's newspapers and magazines were reporting every move in great detail. When Lucille declared, 'I don't care if he is white or black, I love him!' the statement was splashed over the front pages, as was Mrs Cameron-Falconet's riposte, 'I'd rather see my daughter dead than marry a black man.'

Public opinion was outraged. There were hooded meetings of the Ku-Klux-Klan and threats of lynch mobs. Johnson could not walk down a street without being abused. Some 40,000 people marched through Chicago in a great demonstration against the heavyweight champion.

The husband of Adah, the girl who had shot Johnson in the foot, added insult to injury when he sued the champion for alienating his wife's affections. The Illinois licensing board used this to withdraw Johnson's permit to buy liquor. The Café de Champion was closed down.

The police then discovered another former girlfriend of Johnson's, a prostitute called Belle Schreiber. Some years before, Belle had attached herself to the champion and travelled all over the country with him.

Technically this meant that Johnson had violated the Mann Act. This was a statute designed to prevent the white slave traffic, making it illegal to transport women across state lines for immoral purposes.

Johnson was arrested and taken to prison in handcuffs. Lucille Cameron was no longer needed by the state's legal authorities and was quietly released. Johnson was arraigned on a charge of violating the Mann Act with Belle Schreiber. He was tried, found guilty, fined $1000 and sentenced to a year and a day in prison.

The drama was not yet over. Johnson was released on bail while he appealed against the verdict. Instead, he married Lucille Cameron and fled the country. He did not return to the USA for seven years.

# In the Midst of Life ...

## Calgary, May 1913

Luther McCarty was the best of the many White Hopes who surfaced during the reign of Jack Johnson. He even claimed the title of White Heavyweight Champion of the World.

In 1913, he was matched with an obscure opponent called Arthur Pelky in a converted barn at Calgary, Canada. The promoter was Tommy Burns, the former champion. Before the contest got under way and while the fighters were waiting in their corners, Burns asked a local minister to say a few words from the ring.

The clergyman chose as his theme the imminence of death and the need for everyone to be prepared to come face to face with God at any moment.

'In the midst of life, we are in death. Even these huge athletes are not immune. The giants and the weaklings must obey the inevitable law. These men sitting here, awaiting the start of this fight, do not know when they will be struck down. Let all of us, then, resolve to live our lives so that when we are called, we shall not be found wanting.'

These were sombre words with which to herald a boxing match. A few minutes later they proved singularly appropriate. Soon after the contest started, Luther McCarty was lying dead on the floor of the ring.

At the opening bell McCarty had gone at once into a clinch. As they broke free, Pelky delivered a light punch to the other man's head. McCarty crumpled and fell to the canvas in a daze. His eyes closed and he rolled over.

The 10,000 spectators present were convinced that they had witnessed a most unconvincing 'fix'. They were so riled that mounted police had to be called into the barn to restore order.

Then it was announced that the twenty-one-year-old Luther McCarty was dead. At an inquest it was decided that the young heavyweight had died from natural causes, probably caused by a fall from a horse a few days before the bout.

For years a famous photograph was circulated and printed in many magazines. It showed the prostrate form of McCarty caught in a ray of sunshine coming in through the roof of the barn. It is a most dramatic depiction of the event, but today is regarded as a touched-up fake.

# The Iron Man

New York, July 1913

It was the sixth and final round of the bloody bout between Joe Borrell and Joe Grim in New York. As usual the thirty-two-year-old Grim had taken a terrible beating. It was the Iron Man's speciality. The hardened spectators looked on with curiosity. Would Grim last to the final bell in this his last contest?

Somehow he managed it. Borrell's glove was raised automatically by the referee. Grim staggered to the ropes, blood pouring from his nose and mouth. The cynical crowd fell silent, waiting with eager anticipation for the beaten fighter's final valediction. It was not to be disappointed. Grim waved unsteadily.

'I am Joe Grim!' he croaked. 'I fear no man on earth!'

It was a boast he had made on hundreds of occasions. Most boxers have a trademark. With some it is a good jab, others are fine defensive fighters. Joe Grim's selling point was getting beaten up.

Born Saverio Giannone in Italy in 1881, he had come to the USA at an early age and embarked upon a career as a professional boxer. Some reckoned that human punchbag would be closer to the mark.

Grim, his adopted name, could not box and did not possess a hard punch. He could, however, soak up punishment which would have incapacitated a normal man. In the course of a ring career which lasted eleven years and covered more than 300

84

fights, he won only ten fights in an era of no-decision contests. What made Grim a headliner was his ability to last the distance against the most fearsome fighters of his era. Joe Grim was knocked out only three times, twice in the last three years of his career.

It became a point of honour among the hardest punchers of the time to fight Joe Grim and try to put him away. For years none of them succeeded. He fought the greatest champions and contenders of his day and went the distance with all of them – Jack Johnson, Jack O'Brien, Bob Fitzsimmons, Joe Gans, Peter Maher and the Dixie Kid. They all had to be content with points verdicts over the Iron Man.

Grim made little attempt to put his opponents away, but neither did he dodge or run. He stood there, absorbing dreadful beatings in a manner which would not be countenanced today. He was an enormous drawing card all over the world. Crowds would flock to the arenas in which Joe Grim was appearing, thrill as he took his beating and then cheer wildly as he groped his way to the ropes, peered at the spectators through half-closed eyes, and shouted:

'I am Joe Grim! I fear no man on earth!'

# *What's in a Name?*

## Milwaukee, November 1913

James J Johnston, the Liverpool-born hustler who settled in the USA, was reputed to be one of the most persuasive opportunists ever to manage a boxer. These attributes earned him the nicknames of the Man of a Few Million Words, and the Boy Bandit.

It was said that Johnston could sell a refrigerator to an Eskimo. He certainly managed the fistic equivalent by building up the career of a quite remarkably untalented South African heavyweight called George Rodel.

Rodel was fortunate enough to be fighting during the reign of the black heavyweight champion Jack Johnson. Johnson was such an unpopular title-holder that the notorious White Hope campaign was launched to find a white challenger for the championship. This led to the emergence of a motley collection of oversized, clumsy lumberjacks, miners and farm workers. Even amid this fraternity Rodel managed to stand out as being below average.

Johnston could do little to improve his charge's limited boxing ability but he could alter the big man's image. He started by manufacturing a spurious war record for the South African. Johnston claimed that Rodel had been a hero of the Boer War and had been involved in the Siege of Ladysmith. Only some time later did an unkind reporter point out that Rodel would have been all of twelve years old at the end of hostilities.

Meanwhile Rodel placidly posed for publicity photographs wearing a slouch hat, with a bandolier across his chest. He also changed his ring name to Boer Rodel.

So far so good. The main stumbling block still remained. Rodel could not fight a lick. In England he was knocked out in seven rounds by a useful black heavyweight called Sam McVey.

The other white Hopes, however, were almost as bad. They stumbled around beating and losing to one another with no rhyme or reason. The best, or the least bad, of the bunch was Jess Willard. Known as the Pottawatomie Giant he stood 6½ feet tall and weighed 250 pounds. He was slow and cumbersome but did possess a heavy punch. He had actually killed one opponent, Bull Young, in the ring, with a right uppercut.

When James Johnston informed Boer Rodel that he had secured him a match with Jess Willard, the South African had no difficulty in restraining his gratitude. A perceptive man, Johnston realized that he was going to have difficulty in persuading his man to put up much of a fight.

Always a pragmatist, Johnston decided that if he could not raise Boer Rodel's performance, he had better do his best to lower Willard's. Just before the bell to start the first round in their bout at Milwaukee, Johnston marched over to the giant's corner, ostensibly to examine his gloves. As he did so he muttered to Willard:

'Better take it easy tonight, big fella. My guy's got a bad heart. You catch him right and he's likely to die. That will mean a manslaughter charge against you. Don't say you haven't been warned!'

With that the manager scuttled back to Rodel's corner and started massaging the boxer's chest solicitously. The bell sounded to start the fight and both boxers advanced to the centre of the ring.

To Johnston's amazement and considerable relief, Willard actually believed him. The bout which followed was one of the dullest ever witnessed. Boer was terrified of Willard and hardly threw a punch at the big man. For his part Willard scarcely dared touch his opponent in case he did Boer some permanent damage.

Johnston did his best to reinforce the illusion by dashing around the perimeter of the ring for the entire bout, trying to catch Willard's eye. Whenever he managed to do so he would clutch his heart dramatically, like the heroine of a melodrama.

The fight dragged on to its dreary conclusion. It was the era of no-decision contests, but most of the ringside reporters judged that Rodel was worth at least a draw, an unofficial verdict which did the South African's stock a great deal of good.

Unfortunately it also induced Rodel, encouraged by his survival in the first bout, to challenge Willard to a return match.

'Willard ain't so hot,' he told his manager. 'He hardly laid a glove on me last time.'

Johnston did his best to dissuade his boxer, but short of admitting his stratagem, he could not think of a good reason for refusing the proposed contest. Rodel went in with Willard again, this time at New Haven, a month after their first bout.

By this time Willard's manager had heard of the ruse which had made his fighter a laughing stock in the fight game. He managed to convince the slow-witted giant that Rodel was perfectly healthy. Willard knocked Rodel out in nine rounds.

Equally slow in the uptake, Rodel figured that the second result had been a fluke. Willard had managed to land a lucky punch. He demanded a third fight. This time he lost in six rounds.

Willard went on to win the heavyweight championship from Jack Johnson. James J Johnston decided that Boer Rodel did not possess the mental dexterity to reach the heights of the boxing world and allowed the South African to fade away into obscurity.

After all, there were plenty of other reputations to be bolstered. Johnston next latched on to a dull, swarthy Welsh light heavyweight named Danny Thomas. Johnston had the fighter's ears pierced and made him wear gold earrings and a red bandanna. He changed the Welshman's name to Gypsy Daniels and launched him on the boxing public.

# The Kid's Last Fight

## London, March 1914

If the Dixie Kid's mind was not really on his last fight, he could hardly be blamed. Bill Bristowe was hardly in his class and could be put away whenever the Kid pleased. The problem was that as soon as the bout was over a posse of London policemen waited at the ringside to deport him.

The Dixie Kid, whose real name was Aaron Brown, practically originated the phrase, 'Have gloves, will travel!' A superb boxer with a deceptively lazy style, he was an opportunist in and out of the ring.

He was good enough to hold the world welterweight title briefly, stop a future world light heavyweight champion in Georges Carpentier, and defeat three holders of the British welterweight title.

The black fighter first came to Europe from the USA in 1911. The official explanation was that he could not find enough opponents of sufficient calibre at home. In fact, as usual, the Kid was one jump ahead of the law. As one of his contemporaries put it, 'You never knew what Dixie wouldn't do next. He was just a bag of mystery.'

The Dixie Kid spent three years fighting in France and Britain and getting into trouble with the law. When the wraps were off he was practically unbeatable. His favourite ring trick was to pretend to be dazed and groggy and then suddenly ice his opponent with a stiff right as the other man rushed in.

There were times when the Kid lost fights he should have

well won. When he was taxed about this by his manager Charlie Rose, the Kid merely shrugged.

'What can I do?' he asked rhetorically. 'If I win every fight I shall soon be out of work.'

It was his brushes with the law which caused the Dixie Kid more trouble than any of his opponents. He had a liking for young girls, which led to the police moving in on him in London.

The Dixie Kid's last opponent, Bill Bristowe, had outpointed the Kid earlier in the year over twenty rounds in London. With his fighting career practically at an end, this time there was no need to carry his adversary. The Dixie Kid moved in and knocked the other man out in the second round with contemptuous ease. He then surrendered to the law and was escorted to the docks and the first vessel sailing out.

The Dixie Kid ended up in the melting pot of wartime Europe, Barcelona. He opened a disreputable night-club, which failed. Then he tried his hand as a low-grade spy for both the British and the Germans. The former boxer provided so much misinformation to both sides that the British and German consuls united to insist that he be shipped back to the USA. When the Kid died, years later, he was a pauper. A public subscription had to be taken up to bury him.

# University Challenge

## Paris, April 1914

Georges Carpentier, the dashing and handsome French boxer who was later to win the world light heavyweight title, was known as the scourge of British boxers. By the end of 1913 he had knocked out Jim Sullivan, Bandsman Rice, Young Joseph and had twice disposed of the British heavyweight champion, Bombardier Billy Wells.

The second defeat of the British champion particularly rankled with followers of the sport. The big man had been stretched out in sixty-three seconds. Many declared that an amateur could have done better against the French champion.

This thought took hold among a group of Cambridge University students. The Cambridge heavyweight blue was a final-year student called George Mitchell. He was a reasonable enough amateur but had no aspirations at all towards the professional ring.

Nevertheless, a group of wealthy followers of the sport approached Georges Carpentier in Paris. The well-heeled Mitchell was willing to bet £1000 that he could stand up to the French champion for longer than Bombardier Wells had done. Would Carpentier be prepared to take him on privately for a fee of 5000 francs?

The idea appealed to Carpentier and he agreed to box Mitchell in a private room belonging to a boxing instructor in the Latin Quarter of Paris.

Before the bout the earnest Mitchell buttonholed his

adversary and begged Carpentier not to pull his punches when they entered the ring. It would not be the done thing if the champion were to carry his opponent. Solemnly Carpentier promised to hit the Cambridge undergraduate as hard as he could. Equally gravely Mitchell thanked the Frenchman for his sense of justice.

Before a carefully selected group of friends, the two men met. Carpentier knocked Mitchell down with the first punch he threw, and then floored him on two more occasions. Despite the fact that he was dazed and shaken, Mitchell made no effort to retreat and Carpentier punched his amateur opponent as hard as he could.

A great cheer went up when Mitchell was still on his feet at the stipulated sixty-three-second mark. The referee allowed the student to take a further pounding for another fifteen seconds, and then stopped the bout.

Mitchell shook Carpentier warmly by the hand and thanked the professional for the privilege of being knocked about. That night Carpentier happened to run into the bruised but happy Mitchell in the street and spent a convivial evening with the student and his friends.

A few months later George Mitchell, like countless others, answered the call to the colours upon the outbreak of the war, and was killed in action.

# *Four Decisions*

## London, April 1914

Spectators at the Blackfriars Ring in 1914 had no reason to complain at the decision in the Bandsman Blake–Joe Borrell contest. They were given four from which to choose. In fact they did complain, long and vociferously.

Blake was a good British middleweight and Borrell was an American who, erroneously, claimed the world championship. The hall was a sell-out for their contest.

At the end of the fourth round, the bell sounded and Blake dropped his hands. Borrell claimed that he had not heard the bell above the uproar in the hall. He dropped Blake with a crisp punch. The referee, J T Hulls, counted the British middleweight out.

At once the referee was surrounded by Blake's seconds, screaming that their man had been wronged. Hulls allowed himself to be persuaded to change his decision. Borrell had been disqualified and Blake was the winner.

Now it was the turn of the American's handlers to surround the referee, yelling furiously at him. Once again Hulls changed his mind. Neither man had won and the bout would continue.

He reckoned without Blake. The British middleweight remained where he was, stretched out on the canvas. There was no way in which their man could be expected to carry on, said the Bandsman's backers.

There was only one decision left to Mr Hulls. He declared

the bout to be a no-contest. It was his fourth decision of the evening, and the one which stuck.

# 'Tell 'em What I Did to Colin Bell!'

## London, June 1914

Most boxers lose a number of contests in the course of their careers. Usually these losses are soon forgotten. Now and again an unfortunate fighter discovers that one of his defeats has become a part of folklore.

One man to whom this applied was the Australian heavyweight Colin Bell. Bell was an undistinguished but game fighter who scraped a living in the British rings just before the First World War. He managed to secure a contest with the British champion, Bombardier Billy Wells, and encountered the unreliable champion on one of the latter's better nights.

Wells knocked Bell out in the second round with a terrific uppercut which, said spectators, lifted the Australian six inches off the ground before sending him to the canvas like a rag doll.

Soon afterwards Wells joined the army while Bell went to America where he had an unsuccessful series of contests and then vanished from public view.

In the normal run of things everyone would have forgotten the Australian fighter in a month or so, but his name was preserved for posterity in an unusual way. A music-hall comedian called Harry Weldon had been touring with a burlesque act in which he played Stiffy, an incompetent goalkeeper.

Weldon decided to enlarge his act by including a scene in which he came on to the stage as an aspiring boxer.

95

Accompanied by a straight man who played his manager, Stiffy would peer out at the audience and offer to fight any lady in the house. If it looked as if one of the spectators might accept the challenge, Stiffy would cower in simulated fright and beg his manager to 'tell 'em what I did to Colin Bell!' in an effort to repulse the onslaught.

The act caught on, and Weldon toured with it for years. His catch-phrase caught on, and for a long time after Colin Bell had retired from the ring, somewhere someone would be trying to raise a laugh by shouting, 'tell 'em what I did to Colin Bell!'

# The Nephew of Oscar Wilde

## Barcelona, July 1916

In his autobiography Jack Johnson wrote of his period of exile in Spain while he was on the run from a white slavery charge in the USA:

'I also arranged a ring contest with Arthur Craven who was an English heavyweight and had fled to Spain because of the war. A large crowd was attracted by the contest which lasted but a short time, for I knocked him out in the first round.'

Arthur Craven certainly was on the run from the British army, and he did last only a round against Jack Johnson, but there was a little more to Craven and the fight than is recounted in Johnson's terse account.

Arthur Craven had been a prominent member of the artistic world of pre-war Paris. He was related to Oscar Wilde's wife but claimed to have been the dramatist's nephew. Craven had been the editor of an avant-garde magazine entitled *Maintenant*, which adopted a nihilist attitude to everything. To reinforce his reputation for eccentricity, Craven would deliver public lectures on art wearing nothing but a jock-strap.

Upon the outbreak of the war in 1914, Craven fled from Paris when the Germans advanced on the city. He could not return to Britain because that might have meant joining the armed services.

Like much of the human flotsam of the time, Craven ended up in neutral Spain, and made his home in Barcelona. It was there that he encountered the exiled Jack Johnson. Like

Craven, the heavyweight champion was fat, out of condition and broke. They decided to hoax the gullible public by promoting a boxing match in which Johnson defended his title against Craven, who would be billed as a leading British heavyweight. In fact he had never been in the ring in his life.

The fight attracted considerable publicity for its novelty value, and tickets sold well. The bout was actually billed as the Heavyweight Champion of the World versus the Nephew of Oscar Wilde.

The fight took place in an open-air arena on a Sunday afternoon. There was a large crowd expecting an exciting bout. The contest turned out to have been considerably over-hyped. At the opening bell Craven stood up and edged a metre or so out of his corner. Then he bent double, covering his face with his open gloves and protecting his ribs with his elbows. For almost a minute he crouched in that posture, while the crowd screamed for action and Johnson prowled up and down impotently in front of the human hedgehog.

Craven was shaking so much that it was visible from the farthest seats. An acquaintance of the former editor, Blaise Cendrars, wrote:

'The negro prowled around him like a big black rat around a Holland cheese, tried three times in a row to call him in order by three kicks to the rump, and then in an effort to loosen up the nephew of Oscar Wilde, the negro thumped him in the ribs, cuffed him a bit while laughing, encouraged him, swore at him, and last of all, a sudden furious, Jack Johnson stretched him out cold with a formidable punch to the left ear, a blow more worthy of a slaughterhouse, so fed up had he become.'

The referee counted Craven out. Johnson turned to wave to the crowd and found himself almost engulfed in a wave of furious spectators demanding their money back. Fires were lit at the back of the stadium and the heavyweight champion of the world had to be escorted to the nearest police station where he spent the night.

Johnson told anyone who was listening what he was going to do to Arthur Craven when he caught up with the Englishman.

There was no fear of that. Craven had had the prudence to demand his purse in advance. He had used the money to purchase a steamship ticket to New York and was on the high seas before Johnson was even released from gaol.

Craven ended up in Mexico. He even contacted Johnson again, in 1918, saying that the locals were so gullible that he and the heavyweight champion could clean up by touring the country in a series of exhibition bouts. Ever the pragmatist, Johnson agreed, asking for an advance in cash and three first-class tickets to Mexico.

Arthur Craven must have had a sudden memory of that dreadful day in the arena in Barcelona. He never replied to Jack Johnson's letter.

# A Quick Dip

## Toledo, Ohio, July 1919

When Battling Nelson turned up at Jack Dempsey's training camp in 1919, the former world lightweight champion was down and out. He was also extremely dirty and stank to high heaven.

Even the kind-hearted Dempsey would not have the reprobate around until Nelson had taken a bath. Bathing had never come high on Nelson's list of priorities, but Dempsey was adamant. The following day the heavyweight was to fight Jess Willard for the world title and he could do without a human trash can in the camp.

Reluctantly, Nelson borrowed a towel and a bathing costume from Dempsey's manager Doc Kearns and set off in the general direction of a neighbouring lake. Night was falling but there was no doubt that it was going to be a hot day for the fight.

Before long, Nelson came across a complex of iron tubs in which a local entrepreneur was preparing a mixture of lemonade to sell at the ringside the following day. This late in the evening there was no one in attendance.

Water or lemonade, it was all the same to the tired Nelson. He would not be given a bed at the camp until he could assure Doc Kearns that he was clean. Nelson had always been a resourceful man. He had devised the notorious scissors punch, in which he would strike an opponent a vicious blow over the liver and at the same time grip the unfortunate man's side in a fearful grip, twisting the liver as hard as he could.

Battling Nelson dropped his towel and plunged into one of the tubs. Unfortunately the mixture of syrup and water had not yet dissolved and he came out covered in a dreadful sticky yellow mixture.

He made his way back to Doc Kearns with his tale of woe. If he expected sympathy he did not know the Doc. Pausing only to retrieve his soiled bathing costume, the manager banished the former champion from the vicinity.

News of Nelson's midnight dip got around. Although the temperature soared the next day, sales of lemonade were not good. No one could be sure that a particular glass did not come from the vat in which the unhygienic Battling Nelson had taken the plunge.

# Royal Performance

## London, January 1921

Jimmy Wilde was the smallest of all world flyweight champions. His fighting weight was around 7 stone. With his pipe-stem arms and legs, he looked anything but a boxer. In fact he could hit with such devastating accuracy and power that the newspapers dubbed him 'The Ghost With a Hammer in His Hand.'

In order to get fights Wilde frequently had to give away weight. Usually he emerged from these contests the victor, but when he was matched with the American Pete Herman, the Welsh fighter discovered that he had bitten off more than he could chew.

Herman was bantamweight champion of the world until shortly before he defeated Wilde. Soon after his return to the USA, he won his title back again. When he agreed to fight the flyweight champion he made it plain that the lightest weight he was prepared to weigh in at was 8 stone 6 pounds, while Wilde as usual would be a little over 7 stone.

Wilde and his manager assumed that the weigh-in would take place at ringside, immediately before the contest. Herman was having none of this. His contract stipulated that the weigh-in would take place at two o'clock on the afternoon of the bout, some eight hours before the contest was due to start.

For some reason Wilde and his manager Teddy Lewis were not informed of this. Shortly before the contest was due to start, the Welshman asked to see Pete Herman make the stipulated weight of 8 stone 6 pounds at the ringside. The reply from the American's dressing room was swift and emphatic. Herman had observed the letter of his contract; he had weighed in at two o'clock and had no intention of revisiting the scales.

This threw the flyweight's party into a panic. Herman would certainly have had a good meal since weighing in that afternoon. He would now probably weigh around 9 stone. That was far too much weight to expect Wilde to give away.

Wilde sent word to the promoter. Unless the American weighed in at 8 stone 6 pounds before entering the ring, the Welshman was going to call the fight off. Herman would not be budged. He had met the agreed terms. What he weighed now was no one's business but his own.

It was an impasse. The promoter was in a panic. Everything was going wrong with his Albert Hall promotion. Scaffolding for the lights had obscured the view of a number of patrons, who were complaining noisily. The other main event of the evening, between Bombardier Billy Wells and the American Battling Levinsky, had already been cancelled because Levinsky had injured a hand. Already the hall was in an uproar. When the spectators heard that the Wilde–Herman contest was going to be scrapped as well there could be a riot.

To make matters worse, sitting at the ringside was the Prince of Wales, later to become King Edward VIII and Duke of Windsor. It was the first visit of royalty to a major boxing promotion. It would be a disaster if the Prince were to be forced to witness any disturbance outside the ring. Already Edward had climbed into the ring to make a reassuring and well-received little speech. Now he was waiting to see Wilde fight the American.

Pete Herman later declared that it was the Prince himself who went along to Jimmy Wilde's dressing-room and asked him to go ahead with the bout. 'Less than ten seconds he was in there,' declared the bantamweight. 'Then out comes Jimmy Wilde, skipping. He came in the ring, and then the fight took place.'

It is unlikely that the Prince of Wales would so break with protocol as to ask Wilde face to face to carry on with the contest. More probably he let it be known through one of his companions that he hoped to see the Welshman in action. As Wilde climbed into the ring, the Prince certainly stopped him and said, 'Thank you, Wilde – and the very best of luck!'

Wilde wanted the American's weight to be made public, so the MC obliged by saying that the contest was no longer considered as having been made at 8 stone 6 pounds, so all bets on the fight were off.

Herman was far too strong for Wilde from the beginning. He almost knocked the Welshman out in the second round and was on top for the rest of the contest. In the seventeenth round he knocked Wilde down several times, and the referee stopped the fight with the flyweight out on his feet.

Wilde's manager may have been out-thought over the matter of the weigh-in, but at least he had the satisfaction of knowing that he had secured his man's purse of $8000 in advance. The promoter decamped with the rest of the takings immediately after the bout, and Pete Herman never received a cent for his trouble.

# One More Time!

## Various Locations, 1905–22

In the opening decades of the 20th century there were a number of black heavyweights capable of defeating the world champion Jess Willard had he been misguided enough to get into the ring with them. None of the black athletes ever got a chance to fight for the title. Jack Johnson, Willard's predecessor, had been such an arrogant and unpopular champion that no promoter would run the risk of another black heavyweight winning the title.

Consequently there was nowhere in particular to go for such gifted black boxers as Sam Langford, Joe Jeannette, Sam McVey and Harry Wills. No manager would risk his white heavyweight against one of these punchers unless the black man agreed for a consideration to lie down to his opponent.

If they were to earn a regular living from the fight game there was only one course open to the black heavyweights. They would just have to fight one another! This is what they did for almost twenty years.

Again and again the leading black fighters would meet in scattered locations all over the world. Sam Langford was generally regarded as the pick of the bunch. He had lost a decision to Jack Johnson but in his day could be relied upon to whip the rest of the circus.

Between 1905 and 1917, Langford met Joe Jeannette thirteen times in locations as far apart as New York and Toledo. He won four of the bouts, lost three, drew one and fought five no-decision bouts with his opponent. He went in with Sam McVey fifteen times, from Paris to Sydney, with stops at Buenos Aires and Denver and most venues in between. Langford defeated McVey four times, lost to him twice, had four draws and fought five no-decision contests.

Pride of place, however, must go to the series between Sam Langford and Harry Wills. They met no fewer than twenty-three times. They fought in Panama, Tulsa, Vernon, Brooklyn and just about every place that boasted a ring. Towards the end of the marathon Langford was getting past his best. He defeated Wills twice, lost to him on six occasions and they fought fifteen no-decision bouts.

One exception to the coloured circus was the white fighter Jim Barry. Unlike most of his peers, Barry ignored the colour bar, although Langford once declared unkindly that Barry was usually so flaked out on drink or dope that he was in no condition to make out the shape, let alone the colour, of his opponent.

Langford and Barry met on a dozen occasions. Although he lost every time a decision was given, Barry never stopped trying. In fact, much later in life Sam Langford was still aggrieved because once he had bet all his money that he would stop Barry in fifteen rounds, only to see the game white man survive to the sixteenth before dropping for the last time.

Despite the fact that Langford defeated Barry enough times to be able to claim him as a private trophy, the two men hoped to continue their odyssey almost indefinitely. Unfortunately, the wild Barry became involved in a bar-room dispute in Panama and was shot and killed.

Sam Langford continued fighting until he was forty-five. Towards the end of his career he was almost totally blind. In his last contest, against Eddy Trembly in the USA in 1924, the black fighter could only make out the dimmest of blurs in front of him. It was enough. He connected with his right and Trembly went out in the third round.

# Home Movies

## Newark, March 1922

Luis Angel Firpo, the Wild Bull of the Pampas, had a number of drawbacks as a heavyweight boxer. The Argentinian disliked fighting, hated training and was too mean even to pay for seconds and equipment.

Despite this the Bull was a hero in his own country. His tremendous right-hand punch and total disregard for ring science made him a national idol.

It was with extreme reluctance that Firpo left Buenos Aires for the USA, but there was a fatal magnet drawing him north of the border. That was where the money was.

When he reached the USA, Firpo discovered that he was completely unknown to the sporting public. That did not distress the avaricious heavyweight. It meant that no one gave a damn if he wore his clothes until they fell to pieces.

However, there was still the small matter of earning some of those precious greenbacks. There were a number of first-rate heavyweights around, giants such as Jess Willard, experienced pros like Bill Brennan, and above all the lethal champion, Jack Dempsey.

Firpo sniffed and looked around for easier prey. He settled on a third-rate unknown called Sailor Maxted. He secured a match with the Sailor in a small hall in Newark. Maxted was a poor fighter but it still took the lumbering Firpo seven rounds to catch up with his opponent and knock him out.

The promoter of the obscure tournament must have

wondered why the South American heavyweight looked so satisfied as he received his meagre purse after the bout. What no one else realized was that Firpo had arranged for his contest with Maxted to be filmed.

The Wild Bull knocked out a couple of other club fighters while he waited for the film to be processed and made a number of arrangements back home in Argentina. Then, ignoring all offers of further bouts in the USA, Firpo sailed home.

The heavyweight spent almost a year touring the length and breadth of Argentina, showing the film in every town and village of any substance and charging heavily for admittance. At these shows Sailor Maxted was billed as the leading American heavyweight title contender, knocked out by the brave home-town boy.

It was an ingenious ploy and it made Firpo a fortune, with no risk or expense on his part. Argentinians turned up in their thousands to watch their fellow countryman destroy the American hero on celluloid.

It was only with the greatest reluctance, and after just about every Argentinian over the age of fifteen had seen the film twice, that Firpo reluctantly returned to the USA. He had an impressive run there too, knocking out a number of good men before he made the mistake of going into the ring with Dempsey. Even then he got lucky for a while and knocked the champion out of the ring, before Dempsey climbed back in and destroyed Luis Firpo in two rounds.

Yet the Bull was still able to turn his defeat into money. He returned to Argentina for a series of lucrative exhibition contests. The only thing which galled him was the fact that he had to pay his sparring partners.

# A Grand Night for Fighting

## Dublin, March 1923

It is probably no part of a manager's duties to be aware of the national calendars of countries other than his own, but if Hellers, the handler of the Senegalese boxer Battling Siki, had known a little more about current events he might not have taken his charge to defend his world light heavyweight championship against an Irishman in Dublin on St Patrick's Day at the height of the Civil War!

Siki was an interesting character in his own right. Adopted and then abandoned by a French dancer, he had drifted around Europe until the advent of the war in 1914. The sixteen-year-old had enlisted in a unit of the French Colonial Army and had been wounded three times at the first battle of the Marne. He had then been seconded to an American artillery unit, where he had learned to box.

The potential of the heavily muscled Senegalese had been noted by Hellers when he saw Siki in action as a bouncer at an hotel. The manager had no difficulty in persuading the youth to take up boxing, and by 1922 the wild and often comical rough-house fighter had been pitched in with the French idol Georges Carpentier for the latter's world title.

It was supposed to be an easy work-out for the Frenchman, who toyed with his opponent for the opening rounds in order to prolong the bout for the benefit of the film cameras. In the second round Siki connected with a wild punch which stunned the champion, and the Senegalese proceeded to hand out a

109

dreadful beating to Carpentier, knocking him out in the sixth round.

At first the referee tried to disqualify Siki for allegedly tripping his opponent, but when the crowd made it clear that they were having none of it, the original knockout verdict was allowed to stand.

Success went to the new champion's head. He became involved in night-club brawls, paraded through the streets with a lioness on a leash, and was arrested a number of times by the police for irresponsible behaviour.

Even so, Siki was the champion of the world and as such a meal-ticket for Hellers. No one could understand why the manager accepted a bout for his fighter against Mike McTigue in Dublin on St Patrick's Day. The charitable assumption is that Hellers was blissfully unaware of what it entailed.

Mike McTigue was already a veteran of thirty-two, with many hard bouts in the USA behind him. Born on a farm in the tiny parish of Kilnamona, on the west coast of Ireland, he had drifted into boxing after he had migrated to the USA, and had fought such doughty opponents as Harry Grebb and Battling Levinski.

At the time he was matched with Siki for the title, McTigue was considering retirement. He had accepted several fights in England, but was amazed when the promoter of one of them offered him a chance at the world title.

Hellers must have considered McTigue to be over the hill when he studied the Irishman's record and accepted the bout. The manager overlooked the fact that it would be virtually impossible for any foreigner to secure a verdict in such a place at such a time.

It was all the same to Siki. The purse was to be £2000, with £1500 to the winner and £500 for the loser. Siki demanded an advance and actually entered the ring with the money stuck inside his trunks.

By this time Hellers was aware that accepting this bout was not one of the greatest decisions of his managerial career. The theatre was surrounded by screaming partisan fans. Just before the contest began, a bomb went off somewhere outside.

Hellers realized that it would be unpleasant if Siki were to lose this fight but that it would be a great deal worse should he win it.

In the event, the subdued Siki trailed on points throughout a dull contest. Whether he had been intimidated by the atmosphere, or whether Hellers had explained the niceties of the situation to him, is not clear.

McTigue damaged the thumb of his right hand in the fourth round, but continued to dominate the bout with his left jab. In a token effort to get him going, Siki's handlers plied him with gin and then emptied a bucket of cold water over him.

The Irishman was declared the winner on points at the end of twenty rounds. The crowd poured into the ring to carry their new champion on their shoulders. A volley of rifle fire from the adjacent Middle Abbey Street made them scatter, dropping their hero in the process.

# The Town That Died

## Shelby, Montana, July 1923

It was sheer bad luck for the elders of Shelby that at the moment they had a collective rush of blood to the head they should also run into Doc Kearns, the grasping manager of heavyweight champion Jack Dempsey.

Shelby was a dull little town with a population of around a thousand, but it was in the centre of an oil field. As the oil gushed out of the ground, so money poured into the town's banks. Fortunes were being made.

Some of the leading businessmen and civic officials of the town, tired of accusations that they were living in a hamlet floating on a sea of oil, decided to do something to improve Shelby's image and put it on the map.

Someone remembered that back in 1906, promoter Tex Rickard had performed a similar function for the shanty town of Goldfield, Nevada, by staging a fight there for the world lightweight title, between Battling Nelson, the Durable Dane, and Joe Gans.

Rickard had capitalized on the local product by displaying the entire purse of $30,000 in gold pieces in a heavily guarded shop window. The promoter was a great showman and the title bout had been a considerable success for all concerned.

Shelby decided to go one better than Goldfield and stage a bout for the heavyweight championship. At first no one would believe that the would-be promoters were serious, but money talked, especially where Doc Kearns was concerned.

Kearns and his fighter were bound together by bonds of mutual mistrust. Dempsey suspected, with reason, that his manager was ripping him off, but he knew that he depended upon the other man's flair to get him lucrative matches. Kearns was contemptuous of the boxer's mental processes but needed the fighter's championship.

When Doc Kearns met the representatives of Shelby, it was like introducing a basking shark to a group of innocent bathers. Almost before they knew where they were, the city fathers had guaranteed the fast-talking manager a total of $300,000 to ensure that Dempsey defended his title against contender Tommy Gibbons.

Kearns insisted that the first $100,000 be handed over when the contracts were signed. Another $100,000 was to be paid several months later, and the final $100,000 two days before the fight. Gibbons was to be on a percentage of the takings for the bout.

The amateur promoters had no trouble in raising the first payment, but then they began to realize that they had bitten off far more than they could chew. When the time came to hand over the second payment they confessed to the scandalized Kearns that they had less than $2000 in hand, a shortfall of more than $98,000. They tried to persuade the manager to accept a large flock of sheep instead.

City-dweller Kearns told the civic fathers what they could do with their sheep and threatened to call off the bout. Somehow the promoters raised the money. They mortgaged their land and sold some oil concessions.

There was never the faintest chance of raising the third $100,000 in Shelby. The proposed world title fight had turned into a corporate millstone around the necks of the promoters.

Reluctantly, Kearns agreed to settle for the $200,000 he already had and anything else he could pick up from the box-office on the day of the fight. That proved to be little enough. The large, specially constructed stadium was half-empty. Both fighters had to wait in the ring in the blazing sunshine because the referee had gone on strike as he had not been paid. Finally he was persuaded to officiate and the contest

113

got under way.

Dempsey had not fought seriously for two years and Gibbons was not all that good anyway. The champion won the bout on points. Afterwards Kearns, regarded in Shelby as akin to Genghis Khan, was threatened and reviled when he left the ring with the champion. The manager had had the foresight to have a private railway engine waiting at the junction to take him to safety with his entourage. He still had the presence of mind first to raid the box-office and carry off all the available money in two canvas bags.

Shelby was ruined. Several of its banks were forced to close. But the town had achieved one of its aims. The rest of the world certainly knew where it was.

# This Year, Next Year

There have been a number of occasions when there has been confusion over a referee's decision. In 1923, Mike McTigue defended his world light heavyweight championship against eighteen-year-old local hero Young Stribling, in Columbus, Georgia. McTigue had the foresight to insist on his own referee, Frank Ertle, being in charge of the fight.

At the end of the ten-round bout the referee declared the verdict to be a draw. At this several members of the Ku Klux Klan entered the ring and forced the referee to change his decision to a points decision in favour of Stribling. As soon as Ertle was safely out of Georgia, he reversed his decision again and declared that the original verdict of a draw stood.

An even more celebrated example of a muddled verdict occurred at the Ring in London's Blackfriars the following year, 1924.

The two contestants were featherweights, Billy Matthews and Danny Frush. Matthews had been a page boy at the National Sporting Club and fought under the nickname of the Fighting Page Boy. He had claimed the European title after a victory over Arthur Wyns of Belgium.

Matthews was the brother of Jessie Matthews, later to be a leading international stage star, who that year was appearing as a chorus girl in Andre Charlotte's *Revue of 1924*, with Gertie Lawrence and Jack Buchanan. Jessie never saw her brother in the ring, but in her autobiography stated that her main memory of Billy was of seeing him sitting all night in front of a roaring coal fire, huddled in blankets in order to lose weight before a fight.

Frush was a popular East End fighter who had campaigned with some success in the USA. He was convinced that he could beat Matthews and the bout caused a great deal of interest, especially when it was announced that the winner would be matched with the British champion Joe Fox.

There was a full house for the fight which was fought on New Year's Eve. As was the custom, referee Charles Barnett officiated from outside the ring, sitting at the ringside.

Frush dominated the early rounds of the bout, sending Matthews down several times in the opening rounds. On each occasion Matthews jumped back to his feet without taking a count.

In the fourth round Frush sent Matthews down again. This time it looked as if the other fighter would have difficulty in beating the count. Matthews was gamely trying to struggle to his feet when Frush dashed forward and struck his opponent in the mouth while he was still down.

The spectators screamed with fury. The referee left his ringside position and entered the ring. The dazed Matthews was still on the floor but he had grabbed Frush by the ankles and was hanging on grimly.

The referee tried to pull Matthews to his feet in order to continue the bout. Matthews refused to rise but still retained his hold on Frush's legs. The seconds of both men entered the ring and headed wildly for each other. The timekeeper decided to make the best of a bad job and rang the bell to end the round.

During the interval both sets of seconds worked frantically to revive their charges, while at the same time shouting insults at the referee, each side demanding that the opposing boxer be disqualified.

At the start of the fifth round the boxers headed for each other like a pair of stags. They exchanged blows wildly and then Frush fell dramatically to the ground, clutching his groin and claiming that he had been struck below the belt.

Referee Barnett was still in the ring but had not seen the offending blow. He ordered Frush's seconds to carry their man to the dressing-room but said that he would give no verdict until Frush had been medically examined.

The crowd jeered and booed as Frush was carried up the aisle and Matthews hurried towards his own dressing-room. Once the boxers were out of the arena Matthews demanded a second opinion, saying that he would not abide by the decision of the hall's doctor.

Accordingly a second medico was sent for, while the trembling Master of Ceremonies announced from the ring that it would not be possible to give the referee's decision until the following day. In this fashion it was hoped to calm the crowd down. A decision in favour of either fighter at this highly charged moment would cause a riot.

The spectators grumbled but agreed to wait. Another bout was hastily got under way, while in the dressing-room Charles Barnett, the referee, conferred with the two doctors who had examined the stricken Danny Frush.

The following day a notice was posted outside the hall. It stated that Frush had indeed been hit below the belt and thus was a winner on a disqualification.

The note was put up on New Year's Day, 1925. The bout had taken place in 1924 but technically the verdict had not been announced until the following year.

# Once Is Not Enough

## New York, July 1925

When two fighters have just been in a torrid bout they do not usually wish to see each other again for a long time, unless there is a chance of a lucrative rematch. Harry Grebb and Micky Walker were not like that. After fifteen rounds of furious action for the former's world middleweight title, the two men fought again for nothing later that night in a brawl outside a night-club.

Both men stood out as characters in a colourful era. Grebb was dubbed the 'Human Windmill' for his all-action style. He loved night-clubs, hated training, and fought for much of his career with the sight of only one eye.

He became a legend in boxing circles for a series of passionate love affairs with a large number of women. The cheerful middleweight was so ardent that often he would make love to a girl in his dressing-room a few minutes before a contest, trot off to fight twelve or fifteen hard rounds, and then return to the dressing-room to carry on where he had left off!

Walker was every bit as tough. At the time of his bout with Grebb he held the world welterweight title. After his retirement from the ring, he was to earn an international reputation as a primitive artist.

His 1925 bout with Grebb was primitive in the extreme. Both men were renowned for their ability to bend the rules, but true connoisseurs gave the middleweight champion the slightest of edges in this department.

In the seventh round Grebb must have thought that Christmas had come early. Referee Ed Purdy sprained his ankle and was unable to keep up with the fighters or separate them in the clinches. Grebb took full advantage of the occasion, considerably roughing up the snarling Walker, thumbing him in the eye, rubbing the laces of his gloves across the challenger's face, elbowing him and hitting him below the belt.

Walker survived to lose on points and both fighters went back to their respective hotels. Neither was the sort to spend a contemplative evening with an improving book, and as soon as they had recovered both men went out on the town.

At some point during the evening the two fighters met up. They greeted each other without rancour and went on to Texas Guinan's night-club together, where they spent a convivial evening drinking with their hostess Miss Guinan. They discussed everything except boxing and reeled out into the night together.

It was then that Walker committed a social error. 'You know, Harry,' he slurred, 'you never would have licked me tonight if you hadn't stuck your thumb in my eye.'

'You bum!' growled Grebb, no longer good-natured. 'I could lick you with no hands!'

He started to shrug off his overcoat. Walker, always a strategist, later gave it as his considered opinion that this was the biggest mistake Grebb made all night. While the middleweight still had his arms pinioned inside his cumbersome coat, Walker took aim and threw his best punch. It caught Grebb on the side of the head and slammed him into the side of a parked cab.

'That punch would have knocked out anybody but Grebb,' Walker would tell his cronies later with dispassionate candour.

As it was, Grebb rallied and came fighting back. The two world champions put on a ferocious bout outside the night-club until a gigantic policeman called Pat Casey came along and separated them. He threw the champions into separate cabs and ordered the drivers to take them back to their hotels.

'Grebb won the first fight,' conceded Walker afterwards. 'But that second one, that was mine!'

# Come Out Acting!

## New Haven, October 1928

Jack Dempsey had been one of the greatest of all heavyweight champions. Rough, tough and with incredible courage, he had served his apprenticeship fighting for dimes in the saloons of the Mid-West. As a champion he had been the idol of millions.

In 1928, the title had gone, lost to Gene Tunney. Dempsey was at a loose end but hoping to enjoy his retirement. After all, he was only thirty-three and he was not short of a dollar.

The ex-champion reckoned without his wife, actress Estelle Taylor. Miss Taylor was ambitious but not overly talented. However, she was married to one of the most popular men of the era. Surely she could turn that fact to good advantage.

She could and did. The histrionic and effete director David Belasco was about to start work on a new production, entitled *The Big Fight*. He needed a leading man who could fight and, if possible, also act.

Estelle Taylor leapt at the opportunity. If Belasco cast her in the female leading role she would persuade her husband to take the male lead. After all, Jack Dempsey had appeared in several Hollywood serials. The fact that one of them, *Daredevil Jack*, had been voted one of the worst films ever made was ignored.

Dempsey was extremely reluctant to tread the boards, but he loved his wife very much and allowed himself, against his better judgement, to be persuaded.

Rehearsals got off to a bad start when Estelle discovered

121

that her husband was being paid three times as much as she was getting. Matters did not improve when the short-tempered and precious Belasco realized that Dempsey was far from being the answer to a director's prayer. For all his rugged appearance, the former champion had a vocal register which sometimes soared into the soprano range, and he was wooden enough to make a tailor's dummy seem positively animated.

Somehow the show was knocked into rough shape and set off on its pre-Broadway run. It was at New Haven that Jack Dempsey found himself fighting for his life.

The big scene in *The Big Fight* was a simulated prize-fight between Dempsey and another former heavyweight boxer, Ralph Smith.

Smith was a giant almost 7 feet tall and weighing in the vicinity of 300 pounds. The script called for him to be knocked out in the first round, an achievement he carried out with spectacular efficiency as the play continued on its tour. In his autobiography *Massacre in the Sun*, Dempsey commented rather sourly on Smith's proficiency at hitting the canvas to order, wondering how often the big man had done this in apparently genuine contests.

On the first night of their week at New Haven, Dempsey kept to the plan and struck Smith a simulated blow on the jaw. He then stood back to watch the giant milk the moment for all the applause he could summon as he went through his celebrated collapse.

Instead, Smith sailed into Dempsey and caught him with a crushing right cross, sending the ex-champion staggering back. Dempsey almost went down but managed to give the signal to the actor playing the part of the timekeeper to ring the bell.

In the second, third and fourth rounds Smith kept up his furious onslaught, battering Dempsey with a barrage of punches. At first the former champion assumed that his opponent was trying to build up his part by adding an extra two or three rounds to the scheduled one in the script. Not wanting to hurt the big man, Dempsey backed off throughout.

By the fifth round the star of the show had had enough. He

went into a clinch and ordered Smith to go down. The giant responded with a swinging punch that almost took Dempsey's head off his shoulders.

That was enough for the retired heavyweight. He came in under one of Smith's looping punches and hit him in the stomach and then to the head. Smith went down and did not move as the crowd marvelled at how genuine the contest had seemed.

Afterwards the fuming Dempsey marched into Smith's dressing-room, demanding to know why the giant had gone berserk on the stage. Smith apologized, telling Dempsey that the latter had hit him so hard at the start of the first round that he did not remember a thing of what had happened after that.

'I knew just how he felt,' commented Dempsey ruefully. 'I didn't know what I was at out there either!'

*The Big Fight* actually reached Broadway. It flopped.

# The Ambling Alp

New York, January 1930

Before the Italian heavyweight Primo Carnera fought Big Boy Peterson at Madison Square Garden in his first bout in the USA, many sports writers suspected that the contest was going to be a set-up. When the brief and incredible bout was over they were convinced that they had witnessed one of the most blatant fakes ever perpetrated upon the American sporting public. In Carnera's case it was to be the first of many.

The Italian was a giant, almost 6 feet 6 inches tall, although his backers claimed that he was several inches taller. He weighed 260 pounds. Journalist Peter Wilson, who knew him well, said that Carnera was also 'about a yard wide and twice as stupid'.

Carnera was a docile, unambitious man, the son of a stonemason. When he was twenty he was contentedly earning a living as a strong man and wrestler with a small travelling circus. He was spotted at one overnight stop by a former professional boxer who recommended the Italian to a shrewd French manager, Léon See.

See had Carnera tutored in the rudiments of boxing and then launched him upon his fighting career in Italy, France and England. Crowds flocked to see the enormous heavyweight, much as they would have paid to see any freak. For several years Carnera ran up a string of victories over mediocre opponents, mainly by the process of leaning upon his adversaries and exhausting them.

Before long it became apparent to his handlers that Carnera had little but his size and strength going for him. The Italian was placid, could not box, was uncoordinated, did not possess a hard punch, and if struck upon the chin his knees would buckle at once.

This did not deter See from taking his protégé to the USA, where the real money was to be gained. Carnera was an immediate attraction, so much so that the protesting See was at once elbowed out and the Italian's management taken over by a group of gangsters, led by one Walter (Good Time Charley) Friedman. Friedman had close contacts with leading public enemy Owney Madden, so no one was going to interfere with Carnera's build-up.

Actually the big man's new handlers proved a little too enthusiastic in their efforts to grab a slice of the action, because it was later discovered that they owned 105 per cent of their boxer. This meant that instead of earning any money from his fights Carnera was actually in debt before he even stepped into the ring.

Nevertheless, the Italian's backers organized an unprecedented publicity campaign on behalf of their fighter. Everything possible was done to boost Carnera's size and strength. He wore a sleeveless robe, not a dressing gown, in the ring in order to emphasize the swell of his biceps. He was given an over-sized red gum-shield which distorted his face, giving him the appearance of an enraged ape.

Carnera's handlers were hand-picked for their lack of stature, thus exaggerating the height of the towering Italian. In public training sessions, sparring partners were instructed never to hit Carnera on the head, as this tended to knock him unconscious.

The American selected to face Carnera on the latter's debut was a third-rate heavyweight called Big Boy Peterson. The bout was a sell-out, and when Carnera entered the ring he received an ecstatic reception from the crowd. Ring-wise reporters were less enthusiastic. Some of them had heard of Carnera's far from impressive European record. Others

reckoned that no one as big as the Italian would have the speed
or flexibility to be a fighter.

They were proved right in a very short time. When the bell
sounded to begin the fight, Carnera shuffled forward and
pushed out a very slow and very gentle left hand. The crowd
assumed that this was in the nature of an exploratory gesture.
They were wrong. It was the best that the Italian had to offer.

Peterson was not much brighter than Carnera. He was in a
terrible situation. He had been well paid to make the Italian
look good and then go crashing to the canvas the first time that
he received a punishing blow. Should he renege on his
contract, he knew that he would be receiving a visit from a few
of the boys after the contest, with the dismal prospect of a
concrete overcoat and a swift trip to the Hudson River.

The problem was that Carnera showed no sign of being able
to deliver anything that resembled a half-way decent blow.
The giant stumbled unhappily about the ring, pushing out
half-heartedly at his opponent.

Enraged by the lack of action the crowd began to jeer and
cat-call. Peterson was in a quandary. It had been arranged that
Carnera's first American bout would end in a spectacular
first-round victory for Carnera.

The seconds were ticking away. In sheer desperation
Peterson dropped his guard and offered his chin to the Italian.
Obligingly Carnera gave it a gentle tap. At once Peterson leapt
into the air and dropped dramatically to the canvas, where he
lay motionless.

Veteran writer Paul Gallico, who was at the ringside,
claimed that as Peterson was in the act of falling he actually
struck himself on the chin in an effort to add verisimilitude to
the scene. After all, pointed out Gallico reasonably, *someone*
had to hit Peterson.

It was some time before Carnera's handlers dared bring
their fighter back to New York. This did not deter them.
Instead they embarked upon a coast-to-coast tour of the USA
which was to gross more than half a million dollars, of which
Carnera saw practically nothing.

Wherever they went, however, the same problem remained.

It was almost impossible to make Carnera win convincingly. Some less than household names were lined up in the opposing corners. In Newark it was Cowboy Bill Owens (knocked out in two rounds); in Oklahoma City it was Man Mountain Erickson (two rounds); in Detroit the opponent was K O Christner (four rounds); and so on.

Some of these adversaries were paid to take a dive, others were threatened and intimidated by hired thugs. A few of the more stout-hearted refused to go along with the fraud; in these cases more ingenious methods of persuasion were used.

In their bout in Oakland, a big black fighter called Leon 'Bombo' Chevalier not only refused to go down but was still enthusiastically hitting Carnera by the fifth round. At the end of the round someone passed up to Chevalier's second a packet of red pepper wrapped up in a fifty dollar note. The handler was able to take the hint and rubbed the pepper into his charge's eyes, thus rendering him unfit to carry on.

In another contest, a fighter also refused to adhere to his script and trapped Carnera on the ropes, belabouring him furiously. The Italian was not even fighting back, yet his opponent's second, encouraged by the sight of an automatic in the shoulder holster displayed meaningfully by a ringside spectator, rapidly threw in the towel, leapt into the ring and wrestled his amazed fighter back to his corner, thus retiring him from the contest.

Throughout this dismal charade Carnera did not know that his bouts consisted of a series of fixes. The giant genuinely thought that he was knocking his adversaries over with real punches.

Occasionally a doughty fighter could not be bought or menaced, and there are four points losses on the Italian's record over this period, but these ranged over sixty contests. At the end of the travelling circus Carnera won the world heavyweight title in dubious circumstances against Jack Sharkey.

The giant's downfall was as rapid as his rise had been. Deserted by his backers, he took a terrible beating in losing his championship to Max Baer. He then lost to Joe Louis and was knocked out and temporarily paralysed by a young heavyweight called Leroy Haynes. Carnera returned home to Italy on a cargo boat, with very few dollars to show for his championship tenure.

During the war he enlisted in the Snipers' Brigade, helping the Allies, and afterwards made a decent living as an all-in wrestler, an activity in which at least no one pretended that the bouts were on the level.

# The Monocled Heavyweight

## London, May 1931

Boxers have formed a staple ingredient of boys' comics. They have come in many different guises, from Rockfist Rogan, the boxing pilot, to Red Fury, the fighting Red Indian. There have been boxing peers, detectives, scientists and school-teachers.

In reality, of course, the truth has been much more mundane. The majority of boxers have been down-to-earth young men engaged in the hardest sport of all. Yet for a brief period in the 1930s there appeared a heavyweight who could have stepped right out of the pages of the *Wizard* or the *Hotspur*.

His name was Desmond Jeans and he was a character. An adventurer who seldom remained in one place long, when he burst upon the boxing scene in a blaze of publicity he was dubbed the 'Monocled Boxer' for the eye-glass he sported.

Jeans was educated at a public school and was the brother of the actress Ursula Jeans who was to marry Roger Livesey, the well-known stage and film actor, star of *The Life and Death of Colonel Blimp*.

Desmond Jeans had been born in India, where his father was a civil servant, and educated at Sherborne. His mother had been on the stage and the restless Jeans embarked upon a career as a professional dancer as a protégé of the instructor and band-leader Victor Sylvester.

After coming fourth in the world ballroom dancing

championships the wanderlust bug bit Desmond Jeans and he toured Australia in a series of stage shows, with time out to work as a dock labourer and to attempt unsuccessfully to set up a world record for non-stop dancing. Between these activities he managed to win an amateur boxing tournament.

Jeans returned to England in due course to appear in a small part in the West End production of *Hold Everything*, and then was on his way again, this time to New York to appear in *Bitter Sweet*, Noël Coward's great musical hit.

Back in Great Britain, Jeans decided that his acting career was not getting very far. He decided to try his hand at professional boxing. His dancing had kept him fit and he had always been athletic, playing rugby for Richmond.

Desmond Jeans had a flair for publicity and soon the newspapers were full of stories of a mysterious heavyweight who was in secret training to bring the world title to Great Britain.

Desmond won his first two contests, at the Holborn Stadium and in Paris, by knockouts, and won a second bout in Paris on points. With his monocle and glamorous background, he became a great attraction and a dazzling future was predicted for the newcomer.

Unfortunately Jeans began to believe his own publicity, and although little more than a novice he allowed himself to be matched against the gigantic heavyweight Jack Pettifer.

Pettifer had been boxing only a year but had attracted a great deal of attention with his enormous 6 feet 6 inch physique. He had been discovered by a manager washing dishes in the kitchen of Lyons' Corner House in London. He was basically too kind-hearted for a boxing career, but only three years after his contest with Jeans he was good enough to go twelve rounds with Jack Petersen for the British heavyweight championship and to win thirty out of his fifty-three contests.

The Pettifer–Jeans contest attracted a great deal of interest and there were predictions that the winner would go on to great things. The general public made Jeans the favourite, but those in the know predicted that Pettifer, seventy pounds heavier than Jeans, would be much too strong for his opponent.

For once the experts were right. Pettifer bulled the game Jeans around the ring. The monocled fighter, now without his monocle, was in a quandary. The eye-glass was not a gimmick, it was worn because Jeans was genuinely short-sighted in his left eye. In order to see his opponent properly, Jeans had to get close to him, but every time he approached Pettifer the giant inflicted dreadful punishment on him.

The referee stopped the fight in the fifth round when Desmond Jeans was no longer in any position to defend himself. It was virtually the end of the Monocled Heavyweight's fighting career. He went to the USA and engaged in one fight in the Bronx. He lost, being knocked down six times in the process.

With some relief Desmond Jeans gave up boxing. He had a fling at professional wrestling, became a dance-band leader and returned to Britain to enlist as a policeman at the outbreak of the war.

Even in constable's uniform Desmond Jeans retained his monocle and became such a well-known figure in London that he achieved the distinction of being the subject of a piece of doggerel in *Punch*:

Down Whitehall way where the great ones fare,
Where the cars of Marshals and Sea Lords ply,
At a sight most amazing I stopped to stare,
A cop with a monocle fixed in his eye.

# Taking Steps

## Liverpool, October 1931

Professional boxers are constantly on the look-out for an 'equalizer', something which will neutralize the superior attributes of an opponent and bring the two contestants to a state of parity.

Tommy Farr, the old heavyweight, summed up the basic tenet when he growled, 'If the other bloke wants to fight, make him box. If he wants to box, make him fight!'

At the highest levels the balance is finer. Champions have to rely upon the slightest nuance to obtain an edge over their adversaries. Often the advantage comes after meticulous planning and rigorous training. Occasionally it may be the result of pure chance.

Nel Tarleton and Johnny Cuthbert were two of the finest featherweights ever produced in Great Britain. Tarleton was a Liverpudlian. Three times the national featherweight champion, he won two Lonsdale Belts outright and retired undefeated champion of Great Britain at the age of thirty-nine. For much of his career he boxed with the handicap of only one lung.

Johnny Cuthbert from Sheffield was equally stylish. He held the featherweight title twice and went on later to take the lightweight championship of Great Britain.

When, in 1931, Cuthbert was scheduled to defend his featherweight title against Tarleton at Anfield Football Ground in Liverpool, the champion was more than slightly

132

concerned. The two had already fought a scintillating draw in Liverpool and Cuthbert knew just how good the elusive Tarleton was.

'Nella was a defensive fighter,' Cuthbert told me many years later. 'In our first fight I went forward all the time but he kept me on the end of a left jab and smothered all my attacks.'

Cuthbert was not optimistic about his prospects for the return bout. In addition to fighting in his home town, Tarleton was noted for his agile mind. He would have plenty of new tricks to show the Sheffield fighter.

'It was his speed which worried me mainly,' confessed Cuthbert. 'I knew if I could get close enough to him I would be all right, but Nella was a real dancing master. I didn't know how I was going to catch up with him.'

The contest began with Tarleton moving briskly around the ring, flicking out his tantalizing left and darting away. Cuthbert hustled and bustled but the challenger avoided his rushes with ease.

Then, in the opening round, Johnny Cuthbert obtained his equalizer. It came from an unexpected source.

The referee stepped on Nel Tarleton's foot.

It was no ordinary, apologetic pace but a wholehearted, energetic stamp, which made the Liverpool boxer howl with pain and hop on one leg, nursing a set of badly bruised toes.

'We had been in a clinch,' explained Cuthbert. 'I tried to swing Tarleton round just as the ref rushed in to break us apart. He was coming in like an express train and as I sent Nella staggering back off balance, the referee brought his foot down with a wallop, right across poor Nella's toes.'

Cuthbert realized with relish that his opponent had been partially crippled and considerably slowed down. He started to apply pressure at once.

'They called him the dancing master,' he said with grim satisfaction. 'Well, after he'd been trodden on by the referee I made him dance like Fred bloody Astaire!'

For five rounds Cuthbert fought at top speed, forcing his limping opponent to keep pace with him or receive a bad beating.

'We were going round that ring like a pair of whirling dervishes,' recalled Cuthbert. 'Nella was swearing at me something dreadful, and when I wasn't hitting him I was trying to stamp on his bad foot!'

Cuthbert staked everything on catching up with Tarleton while the latter was still hobbling, but although he threw everything he had at his adversary, the gritty Liverpudlian managed to weather the storm.

'I had put too much into those first five rounds,' said Cuthbert. 'I thought with Nella hopping around like Long John Silver I would catch up with him and knock him flat, but he managed to keep out of my way long enough for me to start blowing. Then he came back into the fight, bad foot and all!'

For the second half of the contest Tarleton, ignoring the pain in his foot, came back at the exhausted Cuthbert and even dropped the Sheffield man for two long counts. Tarleton was given a points verdict and the championship.

'Losing the title was bad enough,' sighed Johnny Cuthbert, 'but it didn't half rub it in when I realized I'd been beaten by a bloke with one lung and only one foot!'

# The Wrong Decision

## London, March 1933

Matt Wells had been one of Britain's finest lightweight boxers. He had won the ABA title on four consecutive occasions, and when he turned professional he won the British and European championships. He had his last bout at the age of thirty-six in 1922 and then became a respected referee. One night in 1933 everything went tragically wrong.

Wells was the referee at an international heavyweight contest held at the Albert Hall, between the German Walter Neusel and Don McCorkindale, the heavyweight champion of South Africa.

Much had been expected of this bout but it turned out to be dreadfully dull. McCorkindale did quite well in the early stages but then the ponderous German began to take over and seemed to be well on top at the end of the twelve rounds. There was pandemonium when Wells, the sole official in charge, announced the result as a draw.

So much fuss was made in the press and so many rumours began to circulate about heavy bets being placed on the result, that the British Boxing Board of Control summoned Wells before a special committee to explain his actions on the night of the fight.

It was obvious that Matt Wells had something to hide, but he was evasive and would not answer the committee's questions satisfactorily. He did admit at one stage that he had suspected that the two boxers had not been trying. He was

135

asked why he did not declare the bout no-contest.

'I am an old boxer,' replied the referee. 'I have an old boxer's heart. I could never turn two men out of the ring.'

The Board of Control decided that Wells had deliberately given an unfair decision in the Neusel–McCorkindale bout. They suspended him as a referee. Wells sued the Board and the case went to court.

Again the decision went against the former boxer. In his summing up after a four-day hearing, the judge said that people who paid to see boxing matches were entitled to expect that the referee would be an honest and competent person. He found in favour of the Board of Control.

The scandal of the Neusel–McCorkindale fight did boxing a great deal of harm. In his autobiography, *Come In Barry!*, the referee and radio commentator W. Barrington Dalby gives it as his opinion that it was a definite case of a 'fixed' fight.

# *Retired Hurt*

## London, April 1933

We all have days we would like to forget. Tommy Farr's came at the Crystal Palace in 1933. Farr was an up-and-coming young Welsh light heavyweight. He was brought in at the last moment to fight Eddie Steele of Norwood.

It was a dull fight but it came to unexpected life in the seventh round when Steele jabbed Farr in the throat. It did not seem a particularly potent blow. To the amazement of the crowd and his opponent, Farr suddenly dropped his guard, turned and ran across the ring and dived out of it, sprinting up the aisle to his dressing-room.

Farr never gave a reason for his bizarre behaviour. Perhaps the occasion of a big London fight was too much for the nineteen-year-old. It was a long time before he was given another fight in the capital.

Tommy Farr went on to win the British heavyweight title and give Joe Louis the bout of his life for the world championship. Again and again he demonstrated his courage and durability in the ring.

Even so, to those spectators at the Crystal Palace on that evening in 1933, Tommy Farr remained the fighter who had turned and run away from his opponent.

# Who's a Bum?

## New York, June 1934

Max Baer, heavyweight champion in the 1930s, was more at home on the Hollywood shooting stages than he ever was in the ring. He even made one quite successful film. It was called *The Prizefighter and the Lady*. It was directed by the celebrated W S ('One-take') Van Dyke. Baer played an aspiring young fighter who fell for a gangster's moll, played by Myrna Loy, to the chagrin of the mobster, portrayed by Walter Huston.

The film featured a number of well-known former boxers, including Jack Dempsey and James J Jeffries. The climax came when Baer was supposed to challenge the Italian behemoth Primo Carnera for the title.

At that time Carnera actually held the heavyweight crown and Baer was one of his real-life contenders. During the making of the film Baer began to realize that the gigantic Italian was both slow-moving and slow-thinking, and should not be all that difficult to defeat in a real contest.

Accordingly Baer set out to attain a moral ascendancy over the champion on the set. He made Carnera's life a misery, ruffling the big man's hair and playing 'he loves me, he loves me not' with the hairs on the giant's chest.

In the script Baer was supposed to defeat Carnera, winning the title and Miss Loy. Carnera was so enraged by Baer's attitude that his backers insisted that the ending be changed, so that Baer only drew with the champion.

Convinced that he could beat Carnera, despite the Italian's

fifty pounds' weight advantage, Baer began to take his career seriously for once. He campaigned for a genuine title shot. His reputation as a cheerful playboy made him popular with the public, and the bout was scheduled for Long Island.

Baer, trained to a hair, administered one of the worst beatings ever witnessed in a championship. In eleven rounds he knocked Carnera down twelve times. Once, after sending the Italian tumbling to the canvas, Baer overbalanced and fell beside the champion, crying, 'Last one up's a cissy!'

After the referee had stopped the bout in the challenger's favour, the excited Baer rushed to the ringside and gestured to an official who had gone on record as stating that Baer was not up to much as a fighter.

'Who's a bum now?' roared the new champion.

'You still are,' grunted the unimpressed official. 'But Carnera's a bigger one!'

The defeat of Carnera was the high-spot of Max Baer's fistic career. After that it was back to the high-life for the title-holder. He lost his championship to the plodding Jim Braddock and was then misguided enough to go in against the rising young star Joe Louis, the 'Brown Bomber'. Baer was knocked out in four rounds. Afterwards he was asked why he had not got up when Louis had knocked him down. As usual Madcap Maxie had an answer.

'I figured that twenty bucks entitled people to see a fight,' he explained, 'not an execution!'

# Repeat Performance

## Bournemouth, October 1936

Freddie Mills was to become the light heavyweight champion of the world and one of the most popular of all British boxers. In 1936, however, he was just another youngster trying to break into the fight game.

For his third professional contest Mills was matched with an American living in England, Jack Scott. They met at the Westover Ice Rink. In his usual rugged style Mills bustled straight into his opponent and knocked him out early in the first round.

Both the crowd and the promoter felt that they had not had value for money. When Mills went up to be paid after his bout, he was told curtly that he had not yet earned it. If he wanted to receive his purse he would have to fight Scott again that night.

Reluctantly Mills agreed. He waited for three hours while the other contests were concluded and then, at midnight, entered the ring to fight Jack Scott once more. The long wait had done nothing to improve Mills's temper. As soon as the bell sounded he rushed across the ring and knocked Scott out in the opening seconds of the bout for the second time that night.

# The Loquacious Lightweight

## New York, March 1937

Most fighters have been too busy trying to look after themselves in the ring to have much breath left for talking, but there have been several recorded cases of boxers still being able to summon up a few appropriate words.

After a 1983 bout in Las Vegas, for example, Animal Fletcher had just been knocked out by Juan Roldan. At once the prostrate Fletcher was surrounded by solicitous seconds and medics.

'Can you get up?' asked one of them anxiously.

Fletcher squinted up at his entourage. 'I could if you guys gave me some room,' he replied curtly.

In another fight in the USA, in 1987, cruiserweight Dennis Jackson knocked down his opponent Rick Enis. For good measure he then stamped on his adversary's head. When he was disqualified by the referee, Jackson complained plaintively that he had trampled on Enis merely because there had been nowhere else to put his foot!

The best-known instance of a fighter trying to talk his way out of trouble is that of the Italian Aldo Spoldi in his contest with Henry Armstrong at Madison Square Garden.

Pound for pound, Hurricane Henry Armstrong was probably the greatest fighter around in the 1930s. He held three world titles simultaneously, at featherweight, lightweight and welterweight, and fought a draw for the middleweight championship.

141

Armstrong reached the top the hard way. In his early days, as a so-called 'amateur', he would often fight twice in an evening, selling back his prizes to the promoters.

When he turned professional, life was no easier for the all-action black fighter. In order to get to his bouts he was forced to ride the rods, stealing lifts on freight trains. Between contests he begged his way across the USA, seeking warmth and shelter in the Depression years at the fires of the great hobo jungles, sharing beds in cheap doss houses and lining up for hand-outs at the big city missions.

Often Armstrong would train on nothing but bread and water. He suffered more than his share of dubious decisions against favoured white opponents. Sometimes, in order to survive, he was forced to lie down to fighters he could have disposed of in a few rounds in genuine contests.

Despite all these handicaps, Armstrong began to develop into one of the most energetic and furious fighters of his era, even if he still had to rely upon his shoeshine stand to supplement his income.

His reputation grew to such an extent that at least one champion refused to meet him unless, as Armstrong put it, the black fighter agreed to 'do the business' and lose deliberately.

Armstrong became so popular that singer Al Jolson and George Raft, the film star, invested money in him. Just before he won the undisputed featherweight title in a bout with Petey Saron, Armstrong had what he claimed was the most unusual of his 175 professional bouts.

Armstrong was matched against the Italian champion Aldo Spoldi in New York. Spoldi was a good fighter. A year later he was to win the European championship. Yet against the tearaway Armstrong he knew that he had little chance.

Spoldi set out merely to last the distance against the black fighter and forget all about aggression. In order to do this he decided to rely upon his greatest assets, a pair of strong legs and a persuasive tongue.

For the entire ten rounds Spoldi ran backwards around the ring. At the same time he maintained a breathless line in placatory chat. Armstrong recalled how the Italian hardly stopped talking from the first bell to the last.

'You like spaghetti?' Spoldi would gasp in a clinch. 'Fine, I get my people to make you plenty good spaghetti. Just take it easy, huh?'

A minute or so later Armstrong would catch up with Spoldi again and start hammering his ribs. The Italian would wince, clutch his opponent's arms, look reproachfully at him and then make further enticing offers at a rapid rate of delivery.

'How about some pretty girls? You like the girls? I can introduce you to plenty. Just stop hitting me so hard!'

At the end of the tenth round Armstrong was an easy winner, but Spoldi was the only fighter to go the distance with him that year, a tribute to the power of human reasoning, and the ability to run backwards at a rapid rate.

# The Phantom Fight

## New York, June 1937

Max Schmeling, the German former heavyweight champion of the world, was an earnest man. When he was matched to fight Jim Braddock for the heavyweight title in New York in 1937, he prepared for the contest with great care.

Not long before, the German had been considered all washed-up. Then he had pulled off a stunning upset by knocking out the hitherto undefeated young negro prospect, Joe Louis.

Schmeling had been given the chance to regain his title in a bout with the current holder, the Cinderella Man, James J Braddock. It was a bout which was never to take place.

Max Schmeling became an unwitting pawn in boxing politics. At the time Mike Jacobs, the uncouth former ticket scalper, was trying to become the USA's major fight promoter. The traditional home of American boxing was Madison Square Garden, which was under the control of Jimmy Johnston.

Jacobs's trump card was his control of Joe Louis, generally considered the best heavyweight in the world, despite his loss to Max Schmeling in 1936. Although Braddock had signed to defend his title against Schmeling in New York, Jacobs did not allow a little thing like a contract to put him off.

If Louis could win the world championship from Braddock, then Jacobs would be in top spot as a promoter. Through the good offices of the gangster Owney Madden, he approached

Braddock's manager Joe Gould with a staggering offer. If Braddock would break his contract and agree to defend his title against Joe Louis in Chicago, then the champion and his manager would be paid half a million dollars and ten per cent of Jacob's profits on all world heavyweight championship bouts he staged over the next ten years.

It was an offer Gould could not refuse. He signed up with Jacobs. Then he had to find an excuse for Braddock breaking his word about fighting Max Schmeling. Gould was a Jew. Self-righteously he declared that he was tearing up the contract in case Braddock lost to Schmeling. It would be a disaster, declared the manager, if a Nazi were to win the heavyweight championship of the world.

Schmeling refused to believe that he could be cheated in this fashion. He continued to train at his camp at Speculator, NY, and said that he still expected to meet Braddock for the championship as planned. For his part, Braddock also went into training, but to meet Joe Louis in Chicago on 22 June.

Right up to the last moment Max Schmeling trained for his phantom fight. He turned up as promised on the day of the bout for the weighing-in ceremony at the headquarters of the New York State Athletic Commission. Solemnly he weighed in at 196 pounds and was examined by Dr William Walker.

When the ceremony was over, Schmeling looked expectantly at the officials. Braddock had not turned up. Surely the Boxing Commission must strip the champion of his title and award it to the German.

The embarrassed officials conferred and then announced their decision. They were going to fine James J Braddock $1000 and declare the $5000 appearance bond he had deposited as being forfeited. Braddock was also banned from fighting in the state of New York.

It was a pathetic punishment and everyone knew it. Schmeling stormed out and called an immediate press conference.

'The ruling is a joke!' he declared vehemently. 'It practically legalizes the fight in Chicago, and leaves me out in the cold. What does it mean to suspend Braddock? He's going to fight Louis anyway, and certainly the fight will pass to Louis if he wins.'

The thirty-two-year-old Schmeling's opportunity to be the first man to regain the world heavyweight championship had been lost. The German would have stood a good chance against Braddock. As it was, Joe Louis knocked the champion out in eight rounds.

The following year Joe Louis gave Max Schmeling his chance. In a fight promoted by Mike Jacobs, who now controlled the heavyweight championship, the German was knocked out in the first round.

# A Cutting Edge

London, September 1937

Bill Daly was a tough American manager from Philadelphia. In the USA he mixed with some of the more nefarious characters behind the scenes of boxing in New York. Inevitably in this volatile society, Daly fell out with some of the more violent of his associates. For the good of his health Daly left the shores of the USA in 1930s, and made a temporary home in Great Britain.

Boxing was all that the wily American knew and it was not long before he was managing the heavyweight champion of New Zealand, Maurice Strickland. Daly was to prove a little too over-zealous for the liking of the British authorities.

Matters came to a head when Strickland lost a disputed decision to the German Walter Neusel at Wembley. A British manager might have confined himself to a verbal protest, but Bill Daly came from a tougher school.

Armed with a pair of scissors, the American burst into Neusel's dressing-room. The German heavyweight took one look at the scissors in the manager's hand and promptly dived for safety beneath the rubbing table.

Despite the manager's entreaties to come out and fight, Neusel remained cowering beneath the table. Daly then turned his attention to the German's manager, Paul Damski. The American was in the process of making his objections forcefully known to the other man when the police burst in and overpowered Daly.

The Boxing Board of Control banned Daly from working in Britain. The American returned to the USA, where men were men and nobody would raise an eyebrow at the sight of a pair of scissors being brandished in a manager's hand.

# The Fighting Author

## Key West, Florida, March 1938

In *Fifty Grand* Ernest Hemingway wrote the greatest of all short stories about boxing. It is a brilliant description of how a fading champion manages to outsmart a brash young opponent.

Hemingway was a great lover of boxing. Guests at his home had to be prepared to don the gloves with the famous author. In the Bahamas with his yacht *Pilar*, Hemingway would offer $250 to any dock worker who could last three rounds with him wearing six-ounce gloves. He was very proud of the fact that he had once sparred with heavyweight contender Tom Heeney.

While he was living at Key West, Hemingway became involved in a bizarre scuffle in the ring. He was refereeing an amateur bout at a tournament. One of the boxers was knocked down and Hemingway started counting. The stricken boxer's second threw in the towel. Hemingway kicked it out of the ring and continued with the count. The towel came in again and once more the writer kicked it out of the ring, refusing to accept the token of submission.

This enraged the second wielding the towel. He hurtled into the ring and attacked the referee. Hemingway ducked and countered with a right hook, which made the second dizzy. The writer then held his assailant by the ear until the police entered the ring and arrested him.

'The kid lost his head,' grinned Hemingway to reporters

after the fight. 'He's just asked me if I'll referee a fight he's taking part in next week. I agreed.'

# *Missed!*

## London, September 1938

Jack Doyle, the handsome Irish heavyweight, was one of the most charismatic boxers over to enter a ring. He was charming and erratic, a fearsome puncher but no lover of training. He became famous for his liaisons with a galaxy of stage and film stars. He even married one of them, the beautiful Movita, star of the first version of *Mutiny on the Bounty*.

Doyle's most notorious bout was his first encounter with Eddie Phillips at Harringay. Phillips was a fine boxer but a nervous man. Away from the pressures of a crowd he could box magnificently and could hold his own with anyone in a gymnasium contest. He later secured a niche for himself as a small-part actor in British comedy films, notably *Champagne Charlie* and *My Learned Friend*.

Doyle was a heavy favourite to win the contest and toyed with Phillips for the first round. In the second round the Irishman decided that it was time to end the night's entertainment. He rushed at his opponent, missed him completely and went sailing through the ropes and out of the ring. He failed to get back in before the count of ten.

Later the scandalized Doyle complained that he had been held back by friends of Phillips who had happened to be lurking at the ringside. However, when it was learned that the Irish fighter had held the promoter to ransom just before the bout by refusing to enter the ring unless he was paid an extra £1000, there was scant sympathy for Doyle.

There was a return contest a year later. Again Doyle had all the best of it until Phillips stuck out his fist in a desperate effort to keep the other man at bay. That was just the moment that Doyle had decided to make one of his headlong rushes. He dashed his jaw against the extended fist and crashed to the canvas, spark out.

Nothing daunted, Doyle decided to try his luck in the USA. He was no more successful there. He was matched against the gigantic Buddy Baer, brother of the better known Max. It was the sort of bout, as one cynical reporter noted, that they would only pay to see in California. Baer knocked Doyle out in the first round.

Doyle decided to concentrate on his music-hall singing act before returning to the ring. His notoriety had preceded him. At one theatre he was singing the ballad 'Mother Machree' in soulful style when, from the back of the hall, a disgruntled fight fan yelled:

'Doyle, you should be fighting Mother Machree, not singing about her!'

# The King's Chauffeur

## London, October 1938

Benny Lynch had been the flyweight champion of the world. Many claimed that pound for pound he was the best boxer ever to come out of Scotland. The most that could be said for his opponent, Aurel Toma, at London's Empress Hall, was that he had once been chauffeur to King Carol of Romania.

Lynch had been the greatest until he dissipated his talents. 'It was like being hit with a shotgun,' said one rueful opponent, describing the speed and power of the little man's punch.

In the end Benny Lynch was brought down by two opponents – the scales and whisky. Towards the end of his career he experienced the greatest difficulty in getting down to the 8-stone flyweight limit. He was also an alcoholic.

Earlier in 1938, Lynch had been scheduled to defend his title against the American champion Jackie Jurich at the St Mirren football ground at Paisley. It was a sign of the former idol's increasing lack of credibility with his followers that the ground was half-empty for the contest. The flyweight had let them down too many times.

Their suspicions were well-founded. At the weigh-in Jurich was several ounces under the limit. Lynch was a staggering six and a half pounds over the stipulated weight. He was deprived of his championship on the spot. It looked as if the bout would be cancelled but Jurich, after accepting forfeit, sportingly agreed to take part in an over the weight contest. The

153

American found the weight difference too much for him and was knocked out in the twelfth round, after having been floored several times.

The crowd cheered the plucky Jurich out of the ring and booed their former hero heartily as Lynch sat weeping in his corner. It was practically the end of the road for the former champion. He was persuaded to take a fight with an American, Kayo Morgan. This time Lynch agreed to weigh-in at 8 stone 10 pounds. At the ceremony he was over 9 stone. He paid a forfeit of £500 and was outpointed.

Six days after the latest fiasco, Lynch was due to meet Toma in London. He did not train and went on a prolonged drinking bout. His handlers found him only semi-conscious and bundled him on to the train from Glasgow to London.

Lynch continued to drink right up to the fight. In his dressing-room he demolished half a bottle of whisky. He staggered out for the weigh-in. Again he had agreed to make 8 stone 10 pounds. This time he was at his heaviest ever, 9 stone 5 pounds. Again he had to pay forfeit.

More important, he had to pass the medical examination. He dosed himself with caffeine tablets to sober up and was supported out to meet the doctor. Rumours of the former champion's condition were flying everywhere. Instead of giving Lynch the normal pre-flight medical, the doctor subjected the fighter to a series of sobriety tests. He staggered along a chalk line, touched the tip of his nose with his forefinger, and so on.

Lynch had been tested in this fashion in too many police stations for the examination to hold any terrors for him. Automatically he performed the functions required of him and then staggered back for one last drink before entering the ring.

When he went out to face Toma it was obvious that Lynch was in no condition to fight anyone. He was pot-bellied, shaking and hardly able to raise his gloves. His much vaunted defence was now a travesty. Toma could hit him as he liked.

Lynch took a beating in the first round and stumbled back to his corner at the bell. He confessed to his seconds that his vision was so blurred that he could not even make out the other fighter.

Grimly his seconds sent him out for two more rounds. In the third Lynch succumbed to a punch which was really half a push. He lay on his back as the referee counted him out. It was the first time in his career that Benny Lynch had been knocked out. In a way it was a merciful release, because he could not hear the taunts and jeers of the crowd.

The former champion never fought again. He tried a number of cures for his drink problem, even going into a monastery, but nothing could keep him away from the bottle. Benny Lynch died in 1946, eight years after his encounter with the King's chauffeur. He was thirty-three years old.

# The Cosmic Punch

## New York, September 1941

The prospect of fighting the hard-punching world heavyweight champion Joe Louis was daunting. A whole succession of fighters and their trainers tried to figure out a style which would ensure, if not success, some form of survival.

Bob Pastor succeeded in their first encounter by the simple expedient of running away for ten rounds and taking Louis the distance. By the time of their second bout Louis's handlers had worked out Pastor's elusive style. They instructed the champion to cut the fleet-footed Pastor off in the corners. Louis gave Pastor a terrible beating and knocked him out in the eleventh round.

Arturo Godoy of Chile tried a different ploy. He decided to fight Louis out of a crouch, leaning forward at such an angle that his nose almost scraped the canvas. Like Pastor before him he hardly threw a punch, but he lasted the distance – the first time. In the return encounter Louis straightened Godoy up with devastating uppercuts and stopped him in the eighth round.

Pastor had his speed and Godoy the crouch. Lou Nova adopted the cosmic punch. Nova was a handsome young heavyweight from California with a remarkable ability to sell himself to the press and public. He twice knocked out former heavyweight champion Max Baer but then lost one of the dirtiest fights on record to rotund New Jersey barkeeper Two

Ton Tony Galento. Nova was stopped in fourteen rounds, but later claimed that he had collapsed only out of shock at seeing the decision being given to his opponent.

In fact it was almost two years before Nova returned to the ring, but when he did he ran up a string of victories and became leading contender for Joe Louis's crown.

At the time Louis was considered practically invincible. Something was needed to ensure a full house for the contest. Nova obliged by coming up with his theory of the cosmic punch.

The Californian challenger announced that he had become converted to the philosophy of yoga and that he was adapting the principles of this cult to the art of boxing. He lived on raw vegetables, did exercises while hanging from a tree and spent hours strengthening his stomach muscles.

Under the guidance of his mentor, Doctor Pierre Barnard, known to the irreverent as 'Oom the Omnipotent', Nova announced that his cosmic punch was connected with the movement of the earth. The heavyweight was vague about the details, but claimed that when delivered under certain planetary conditions the blow would destroy any opponent, even Louis.

The idea caught the fancy of the public. Some 56,000 spectators turned up at the New York Polo Grounds to see if Nova could enlist the aid of the occult against the all-conquering Louis.

Nova accepted the full house as being only his due. He claimed that after he became champion he would insist upon the return of the million-dollar gate for all his title defences.

Alas, the so-called cosmic punch turned out to be no more than a rather ordinary right cross. A jaundiced reporter wrote that it was more comic than cosmic. Louis did the usual demolition job on his challenger and knocked him silly in the sixth round.

Afterward Nova apologized for his lack of success. He claimed that the earth had been out of position for the effective delivery of his famous blow.

Joe Louis was more down to earth. 'Cosmic punch?' he asked scornfully in his dressing-room. 'Shit!'

157

# Below the Belt

Jack Roper was a very competent heavyweight boxer who had the misfortune to be at his peak during the reign of the legendary champion Joe Louis. Louis knocked Roper out in the first round of their title bout, but at least the challenger was to have the satisfaction several years later of flooring film star and noted off-screen lover Errol Flynn.

Roper fought Louis for the latter's world heavyweight championship in Los Angeles in April 1939. Louis respected his challenger, describing him in his autobiography as 'a hell of a left hooker!'

While it lasted, their bout was an exciting one. Roper was a southpaw, boxing with his right fist and foot extended. In an effort to confuse the champion he kept switching from the southpaw to the more orthodox stance.

His ploy was to prove a little too effective. The hard-hitting Louis decided that he had better put his tricky opponent away quickly, before matters became too puzzling.

Accordingly Louis went after Roper, who fought back with a will. He caught the champion with several good punches before Louis landed with his own right hook. Roper went down and did his best to pull himself back to his feet, but fell forward on his face again as the referee reached the count of ten.

Afterwards Roper achieved a degree of fame for his answer when a post-fight radio interviewer asked the dazed challenger what had gone wrong.

'I zigged when I shoulda zagged,' replied Roper ruefully.

In 1941, Roper managed to secure a few weeks' work on the motion picture *Gentleman Jim*, starring Errol Flynn. This was a highly coloured account of the life of former heavyweight champion Jim Corbett. Flynn always declared that this was his favourite film, and it is one of the better Hollywood boxing biopics.

Roper played the part of one of Corbett's opponents in the latter's rise to fame. At the time Flynn was so out of condition that he could only box in the fight sequences for one minute at a time, so these had to be carefully choreographed.

For once Flynn took great care over his performance and spent a great deal of time with Roper in an attempt to perfect their fight sequences. Unfortunately the old heavyweight did not prove a quick study. At the first rehearsal he mistimed a blow and knocked Flynn unconscious.

The star was determined to persevere. When he came round, he approached the mortified Roper and patiently explained the correct sequence of punches to be delivered before the cameras. Roper promised to follow his instructions to the letter and the director called for action again.

The second take was no more successful than the first had been. When the bell went, Roper forgot all that he had learnt at the rehearsal, sailed across the ring and knocked Flynn out again.

This time it took the film star longer to come round. When he did he staggered back on to the set with a bottle of champagne and two glasses. He poured one glass for Roper and one for himself. For the third time he explained the correct order of the four punches Roper was supposed to deliver. Then he pointed at the champagne bottle and promised to break it over the fighter's head if anything went wrong this time.

The threat had the wrong effect upon the heavyweight. At the start of the third take Roper was so intimidated that he refused to attack Flynn. Instead he stood cowering in his corner.

With the director screaming for action, Flynn decided that desperate measures were called for. In an effort to stir Roper into action the film star moved forward and punched him viciously below the belt. 'I hit him,' as Flynn later recalled, 'right in the nuts.'

Roper's reaction was swift but counter-productive. Automatically he responded with a tremendous punch which lifted Flynn off his feet and sent him crashing to the floor for the third time that day, to be carried back to his dressing-room.

'I loved making that picture,' said the street-fighter Flynn affectionately.

# Come Out Fighting!

## Dublin, August 1945

In the heady opening months of peace following the Second World War, Bruce Woodcock was a hot property in British boxing. The young Doncaster-based railway worker had just won the British heavyweight title by knocking out Jack London in six rounds, and was being steered towards a shot at the world championship.

With his jarring left hand and clubbing right, Woodcock had cut a swathe through most of his domestic rivals. In his entire professional career only one opponent had managed to last the distance with him.

Finding credible opponents, or indeed any opponents for the new British champion in the build-up towards his international aspirations, was proving a headache for Woodcock's manager Tom Hurst. In the end, promoter Jack Solomons managed to persuade the Irish heavyweight champion Martin Thornton to accept the match in Dublin for a purse of £800.

Thornton had already fought Woodcock once several years previously and had been stopped at the end of the second round. Nothing that he had done in that encounter suggested that he would perform any better in a return contest.

Martin Thornton came in the great tradition of Irish heavyweight boxers, being impetuous, flamboyant, hard-punching and not overly talented. If he landed one of his wild haymakers early on, he could knock an opponent into dreamland. However, should the other boxer start to fight back, the gregarious Irishman was apt to lose a little of his enthusiasm.

Thornton took the second bout with the menacing Woodcock purely for the not inconsiderable sum of money involved. It was not long before doubts began to set in. As the day of the fight approached he grew increasingly apprehensive and withdrawn.

Woodcock had no such worries. He was taken to his Dublin hotel in an open, horse-drawn coach while a cheering crowd of 30,000 lined the route. Flowers were thrown at the British champion and he went on to a civic reception at the city hall. Thornton was not involved in any of these festivities.

The bout was held at the Theatre Royal and was a sell-out. Both boxers arrived and changed in their dressing-rooms, and then Thornton dropped his bombshell. He sent for promoter Solomons and announced sullenly that he would not enter the ring unless he was paid the full amount of his purse money in advance.

A shrewd operator in his own right, and a very careful man with a dollar, Solomons was aghast. Indignantly he refused to hand over any cash until Thornton had fought Woodcock. The Irishman merely shrugged indifferently and sat where he was: no money, no fight.

In the meantime, the preliminary bouts had ended and the crowd was waiting impatiently for the long-anticipated main event. When there was no sign of either fighter, the spectators began to mutter and stamp their feet ominously.

Back in the dressing-room the dispute still raged, with more and more officials becoming involved as they pleaded with the Irishman, for the honour of his country, to go ahead with the scheduled contest.

Thornton was obdurate. An onlooker later reported that at one stage the Irish champion even locked himself in the lavatory and refused to come out.

The boxer had the promoter over a barrel and both of them knew it. With great reluctance, Solomons finally handed over the £800. Almost as reluctantly, but with a certain grim satisfaction, Thornton left the dressing-room and made his way to the ring.

The actual contest was a considerable anti-climax. For the brief duration of the bout Thornton hardly threw a blow in anger. He buried his chin beneath his shoulder and retreated rapidly around the ring while Woodcock pursued him with stiff left jabs.

For two horrendous rounds Woodcock chased and Thornton ran. The enraged crowd jeered and hooted, demanding that Thornton stand and fight. At last, in the third round, the Irish champion made his most positive contribution to the contest. He stood still and stuck out his tongue at his opponent!

Thornton then turned to the referee, Andy Smythe, and demanded that the official stop the bout. Gruffly Smythe refused and insisted that Thornton fight on. Thornton promptly retired. His seconds then threw in the towel, a slightly superfluous gesture considering all that had gone before.

Thornton left the ring hurriedly amid a shower of obloquy and empty bottles. The Eire boxing authorities subsequently stripped him of his title and suspended him from the ring. They were unable to withhold his purse because Thornton had had the foresight to collect it in advance from the promoter.

Bruce Woodcock went on to defeat most British and European fighters put into the ring against him, but came to grief against leading American heavyweights like Tami Mauriello and Joe Baksi. He never won the world championship.

Both men later adopted the traditional vocation of retired champions and became publicans. Martin Thornton had one final fling with fistic fame. He was the stand-in for Victor McLaglen in the famous fight scene with John Wayne in John Ford's film, *The Quiet Man*, and may be glimpsed brawling with the star in some of the long-shots.

It was a much more entertaining fight than either of his bouts with Bruce Woodcock.

# The Bronx Bull

## New York, November 1947

Jake LaMotta was in trouble. The tough Bronx middleweight was fighting an undefeated black light heavyweight, Billy Fox, before a crowd of 20,000 at Madison Square Garden. LaMotta was generally considered the uncrowned middleweight champion of the world, while Fox was on a roll of forty-three consecutive winning fights, all of them on knockouts.

It should have been a spectacular contest, but it turned out to be anything but exciting. The trouble was LaMotta had accepted a bribe to lose to Fox. As early as half-way through the first round, LaMotta later claimed, he discovered that the coloured fighter was so inept that he could think of no convincing way of throwing the fight.

LaMotta had a tough background. Born in the slums of the East Side of New York, he had fought his way to the top of his block and then followed the natural route for a successful street fighter and become a professional fighter.

By 1947, the aggressive Bronx Bull had won over sixty contests, including a points decision over the great Sugar Ray Robinson, the first defeat ever handed out to the legendary welterweight. But without a manager or any connections, LaMotta seemed to be getting nowhere. He could not secure a match for the world title.

It was then that he accepted a fight with Billy Fox, who was being groomed for the top by his connections. A number of underworld characters had an interest in the Philadelphia fighter, including the notorious 'Blinky' Palermo, Fox's manager, and the mobster Frankie Carbo.

The first LaMotta knew that he was in over his head against Fox was when his own brother Joey approached him and said that there was $100,000 in it for the middleweight if he would lie down to his opponent in the Garden fight. The implication was that the bribe had come from Carbo and Palermo.

According to LaMotta, he rejected the offer self-righteously. It was not until he had suffered a bad injury in training that he began to reconsider the situation. After a torrid sparring session, LaMotta claimed, he sustained a ruptured spleen. The injury was so bad that he knew he would have difficulty going ten rounds against a reasonably good opponent.

Accordingly the fighter empowered his brother Joey to reopen negotiations with the mobsters. Carbo and Palermo visited LaMotta at his New York night-club and agreed on terms. The meeting took place four days before the bout with Fox and it was confirmed that LaMotta would go down in exchange for $100,000 and a shot at the world middleweight championship at a later date.

LaMotta kept his side of the sordid bargain, but the scheme began to founder when rumours circulated that the fix was in. The bookies covered their backs and it was almost impossible to get down a bet of any substance.

The fight was a farce. LaMotta hit Fox with a couple of sighting shots to make things look good, and then saw to his horror that his opponent was rocking on his feet. LaMotta had to dive in and hold the other fighter upright until Fox's head cleared.

By the fourth round the crowd's suspicions had turned to certainties. They were booing and screaming and demanding their money back as the two boxers played out the charade in the ring. Finally, in desperation, LaMotta backed on to the ropes and dropped his arms to his sides, allowing Fox to hit him at will.

Even then the black fighter could not hit his adversary hard enough to put him down. LaMotta started weaving and

165

staggering in an effort to simulate extreme exhaustion. At last the referee moved in and stopped the contest in favour of Fox.

There was an immediate investigation by the Boxing Commission. LaMotta was able to save himself by providing his doctor's diagnosis of a ruptured spleen. He claimed that he had been in such pain from this injury that he had been unable to fight properly against Fox.

The Commission did not believe the fighter's testimony, but was unable to prove anything. In the end LaMotta escaped with a $1000 fine and a seven-month suspension for failing to report an injury. However, the bout with Fox had been so unsavoury that there was no possibility of his being given a shot at the world title, and LaMotta had to wait another eighteen months for the fuss to die down before he received his reward for throwing the fight to Fox.

Even then it was not all plain sailing for the Bronx middleweight. When a contest with Frenchman Marcel Cerdan for the world title was mooted, LaMotta's ubiquitous brother Joey turned up again. He hinted that his underworld connections were taking a keen interest in the bout and that they needed $20,000 to make sure that the contest went ahead.

The trusting LaMotta gave his brother the money, although he was only getting $19,000 for the bout. It thus cost him $1000 to win the title from Cerdan, who retired with an injured shoulder after ten rounds. LaMotta made up the shortfall by betting on himself to win.

When Senator Estes Kefauver conducted a Senate investigation into boxing, enough people remembered the LaMotta–Fox fight to put this high on the list of bouts to be looked into. By this time the Bronx Bull had retired and was working as a night-club comic and small-part actor. He readily admitted that he had thrown the bout to Fox in order to secure a tilt at the world title. He explained about his poor physical condition before the fight and told the investigating committee, 'When I realized that I couldn't possibly win, I said I would lose to Billy Fox, if I was guaranteed a championship fight.'

# A Weight on His Mind

## Belfast, March 1948

A championship is a lucrative acquisition for any fighter. It can mean prestige, enhanced purses and top billing. Few boxers willingly dispense with their titles. For many of the smaller men, however, it means a constant battle with the scales.

A very good flyweight champion of the world was Jackie Paterson of Scotland. He won his title by knocking out the highly regarded Peter Kane in a single round in 1943.

But Paterson's rangy frame was never intended to support the 8-stone flyweight limit. Not long after he had won the championship he was fighting at bantamweight and even featherweight. Indeed, many experts were convinced that the Scot was at his best at the 9-stone featherweight limit.

Nevertheless, Paterson refused to discard his world championship. For twenty months he boxed at weights much above the 8-stone limit. Constantly he ignored the challenges of the genuine little men.

Eventually the Board of Control insisted on Paterson defending his title against Dado Marino of Hawaii, the first grandfather to challenge for a world championship. Paterson collapsed just before the weigh-in. Many were convinced that the champion's attempts to lose a lot of weight had made him ill, or that the collapse had just been a diplomatic way to avoid disclosing his true weight.

In any case, the Board deprived Paterson of his title. The

Scot at once went to court and was reinstated. Obviously things could not go on like this. Paterson was presented with an ultimatum – defend his crown against a legitimate challenger or forfeit it for ever.

Paterson knew that there was no way in which he could boil off a stone in weight and still remain strong. He had two choices: either give up his championship, or 'sell' it to the highest bidder by making the weight somehow and going into the ring weak and exhausted.

Paterson chose the second alternative and signed to meet the Irishman Rinty Monaghan at the King's Hall, Belfast. Monaghan was a spirited battler, mainly renowned for his rendition of 'When Irish Eyes Are Smiling' after a bout.

Somehow Paterson had to reduce his weight to 8 stone, or forfeit the title and a large purse. With a day to go he was still considerably overweight. There was nothing else for it. For the entire night before his title defence, instead of sleeping, Jackie Paterson was in a sweltering room with a blazing stove, encased in woollen clothing and alternately skipping and playing cards with his friends.

This dreadful penance was exacted until shortly before Paterson was due to weigh-in at Belfast. At the last possible moment the Scot's party left Glasgow in a small aircraft. The champion was late arriving but he just made the weight.

Of course he was as weak as a kitten and had no chance against the aggressive Irishman. Monaghan knocked Paterson out in the sixth round.

Paterson had another dozen contests, losing more than he won, and then made his home in South Africa. He was killed in a bar-room brawl.

# A Fighter in Love

## Paris, May 1948

Boxing and romance do not as a rule go together. However, in France not long after the Second World War, one relationship began to hit the headlines, to the annoyance and chagrin of both principals.

The fighter concerned was the French-Algerian middleweight Marcel Cerdan, a former butcher from Casablanca. Cerdan was one of the hardest-punching boxers ever to come out of Europe. By the end of 1947, he had won over one hundred contests, the majority of them by knockouts, and lost only two, both of them on fouls.

The lady in the case and the object of the middleweight's attention was the famous café singer Edith Piaf. The diminutive star had enjoyed a turbulent love life and had the gift of putting all her heartache into her plaintive voice. When Cerdan first met her Piaf and her accompanying group, Les Compagnons de la Chanson, had just scored an enormous international hit with the song 'Les trois cloches' ('The three bells').

From their first meeting at the Club des Cinq, the boxer and the singer fell in love. They had similar backgrounds. Both came from poor homes and had fought their way to the top. They became inseparable companions and lovers. Cerdan would spend his evenings at the clubs and theatres where Piaf was singing, while the star attended most of the middleweight's contests.

Their liaison was the subject of gossip all over France, but the two lovers were essentially private people and did not want the affaire made public. The newspaper reports came at a bad time for the fighter and led to some strange repercussions.

In May Marcel Cerdan was in the depths of depression. He had just lost his first contest in ten years, dropping a fifteen-round points decision to the Belgian middleweight champion Cyrille Delannoit in Brussels. With the decision Cerdan also lost his European championship.

Boxing fans in France could hardly believe the news. Cerdan had been considered virtually unbeatable; he had already been matched with Tony Zale for a world title shot in the USA. After the initial shock, the newspapers turned on their former hero, accusing him of being arrogant and taking Delannoit too lightly.

The hitherto all-conquering Cerdan was not accustomed to criticism. The public's condemnation of his performance in Brussels depressed him. The last straw came when the newspaper *France-Dimanche* ran a short piece about the way in which the fighter had been seeing Edith Piaf every day on a recent visit to New York, where the singer had been appearing in cabaret at the Versailles and Cerdan had won three fights on a tour of the USA.

The offending article was innocuous enough but it inflamed the already irritable middleweight. Cerdan was a man capable of inspiring great loyalty in his friends, so while the fighter decided to deal with the reporter he considered responsible for the item in the newspaper, his manager Lucien Roupp and the latter's assistant Jo Longman said that they would take on the editor of the *France-Dimanche*.

Roupp and Longman swung into action first. They stormed into the offices of the newspaper's editor, Max Corre. Caution then began to set in when they discovered that Corre was a heavyweight weighing some 200 pounds. At once Lucien Roupp's managerial instincts reasserted themselves. Instead of attacking Corre, as had been his intention, he ordered Longman to do so instead.

The assistant manager was more accustomed to sending Cerdan out to do battle than in participating in brawls himself.

He showed a marked lack of enthusiasm as he advanced in gingerly fashion on the gigantic editor. He aimed a few desultory blows in the general direction of Corre, who responded with a will.

From his self-appointed corner position Roupp poured scorn on his assistant's efforts. He ordered Longman to smarten up his style. Members of the staff of the newspaper separated the two men with no effort. The only damage sustained turned out to be a broken finger where Max Corre had punched his assailant on the head.

The first part of the scheme could not be considered a resounding success. In fact, a week later Longman rang the *France-Dimanche* to make his peace with the editor.

Having sent out his acolytes to carry out the initial move, Cerdan could now hardly withdraw from the second phase. After the wave of mocking publicity following upon the encounter between Jo Longman and Max Corre, the fighter's heart could scarcely be said to be in the project any more.

Nevertheless, he invited the reporter he suspected of being behind the article round to Edith Piaf's Paris apartment. The writer in question, Georges Cravenne, must have had a greater sense of curiosity than prudence, because he duly presented himself at the flat in Leconte de Lisle.

Marcel Cerdan was waiting for him. He greeted Cravenne with a punch. It must have been a token affair, because the reporter was still on his feet after it had been delivered. Cravenne turned and walked away, which was more than sixty of the middleweight's opponents had been able to do after experiencing Cerdan's left hook.

The matter blew over. Two months later Cerdan regained his European title from Cyrille Delannoit. Two months after that he knocked out Tony Zale in twelve rounds in Jersey City to win the world championship.

In 1949, the Frenchman lost his title to Jake LaMotta, when he damaged his shoulder and was unable to carry on after the ninth round. Cerdan and Jo Longman were killed when their aircraft crashed on their way back to the USA for a return bout with LaMotta. Edith Piaf was one of the many mourners.

# Up and Down

## Johannesburg, December 1950

Vic Toweel was one of the most successful boxers to come from South Africa. As an amateur he lost only two of almost 200 bouts, winning 160 of them by knockouts. He won the world championship as a professional bantamweight by knocking out Manuel Ortiz in only his fourteenth fight.

When it was announced that he was to defend his title against Britain's Danny O'Sullivan, everyone expected to see a feast of boxing. O'Sullivan came from a fighting London family and was one of the greatest stylists to grace the post-war ring.

Although perhaps a little too trusting at times, he was knocked out only once in his life, by Jackie Paterson, the former world flyweight champion. I could never understand why such a clever defensive boxer as O'Sullivan could have been caught by Paterson, who was coming to the end of his career at the time. I once asked the bantamweight what had happened. Danny grinned and shook his head.

'I came back to my corner at the end of the sixth round,' he said. 'They told me I was well on top and that I was to go in and finish him off in the next round. I said, "Wait a minute, he can bang a bit, he caught me with one just then." They told me, "Nah, he can't punch. Go in and finish him off!" So I dived in and he pulled one up from the floor and knocked me spark out!'

By the time he fought Vic Toweel, O'Sullivan was having

172

trouble making the weight. He put up a courageous display but set up a record for a world championship bout by being knocked down no fewer than twenty times in the ten rounds that the fight lasted. The referee stopped the contest to save a very brave man from further punishment.

# The Dirtiest Fight

## New York, September 1951

There have been many nominations for the accolade of the world's dirtiest title fight. By general consensus, in modern times the most rules were broken in the fourth encounter for the world featherweight championship between Sandy Sadler and Willie Pep.

The first two contests had been wild. After the second, Pep was asked what his tactics had been.

'I hit him low and he didn't say a thing,' reported Pep. 'I caught him with an elbow and I didn't get a flicker. Then I trod on his toes and he swore at me. So I trod on his toes all night!'

The third match between them was a satisfactory warm-up for their all-in final encounter. In this 1950 bout Pep, a master-boxer, had dominated the opening rounds, despite taking a count in the third. Going into the seventh round the challenger was well ahead. At a press conference afterwards, Pep described what happened then:

'He got a double arm-lock on me in that last clinch on the ropes. I felt a crack in my shoulder and couldn't raise my arm when I went back to my corner.'

Pep was forced to retire after the seventh round with a dislocated shoulder. He was allowed a year in which to brood on the apparent injustice, and then the two men met for the fourth and last time at the New York Polo Grounds before a crowd of 14,000. Later the staid *New York Times* was to sum

174

up the bout succinctly:

'For roughness, disregard of ring rules and ethics, and wild fighting, this surpassed anything seen in the previous three meetings of these bitter ring rivals.'

Referee Eddy Miller caused an unintended laugh at the beginning of the bout as the two hard-cases came out to shake hands, by greeting them with a courteous, 'Good evening, gentlemen.' After that everything went. The featherweights spat, punched low, hit and held, butted, gouged, knocked the referee down and wrestled. At one stage they even stood toe to toe in the centre of the ring and tried to strangle each other.

Reporters later compared the fight to a waterfront brawl in which every rule in the book was broken at least twice. The contest ended at the end of the ninth round when Pep, one eye closed, retired. Even here there was controversy when one of Pep's seconds screamed at the referee to make his fighter go on. For a second it looked as if Pep was going to start another punch-up, this time with his excited handler.

As a result of the bad publicity following the bout, Sadler was suspended from the ring for sixty days and Pep received a suspension for life. He was reinstated several years later.

Both fighters were still bitter after the hearing. Pep blamed the referee:

'It seemed like there was no referee in the fight. He was getting in too late to break us up. The only way I could get away from Sadler was to wrestle him. He was holding me by the head and banging away at my eyes!'

Sandy Sadler said, 'I thought I fought a clean fight!'

# Called to the Bar

Many male film stars claim to have included a spell as a professional boxer in their early years, before achieving fame and fortune. It is the sort of glamorous and usually unverifiable boast which adds a little spice to publicity handouts.

One of these actors is the lugubrious hero of *The Sundowners* and *Heaven Knows, Mr Allison*, Robert Mitchum. It is uncertain whether he really did, as he claims, have a handful of paid fights during the period he spent on the road as a hobo. It is certain that by 1951 any professional boxing career that the thirty-four-year-old Mitchum may have had was a long way behind him. However, it was then that the truculent star had one final encounter which was to hit the headlines.

It took place in the Red Fox Bar of the Alamo Hotel in Colorado Springs. Mitchum was on location there to make *One Minute to Zero*, a Korean war melodrama, with Ann Blyth. They were filming in bitterly cold temperatures at a height of 6000 feet above sea-level.

After shooting one evening, Mitchum was drinking hot buttered rum at the bar with his co-star Charles McGraw. The latter became engaged in a dispute with a young soldier from neighbouring Camp Carson.

The soldier, in fact, was Bernie Reynolds, who not only played football for his unit but had been only recently a rated heavyweight fighter. He had lost only two of almost thirty bouts and had been a stable companion and sparring partner of Gus Lesnevich, the former world light heavyweight champion.

The cause of the altercation was never made clear. Reynolds and McGraw suddenly started pushing one another. Mitchum promptly moved in to protect his friend. 'I was aggressive,' he later admitted, 'but only in the way that a policeman is aggressive.'

Mitchum grabbed the soldier by the lapels. Reynolds pulled himself free and swung a wild right. Mitchum ducked and countered with a right of his own. Reynolds fell to the floor and the film star dived on top of him.

The struggle which followed would not have disgraced one of Mitchum's action films. In the process the two participants managed to destroy a table and knock over a piano.

When onlookers finally parted them, Mitchum staggered to his feet, but the prostrate Reynolds was unconscious on the bar floor. Two eye-witnesses claimed that for good measure Mitchum then kicked Reynolds, but the actor denied this.

The soldier was carried out on a stretcher and taken by ambulance to a local military hospital. Mitchum walked out of the hotel under his own steam.

No charges were pressed against Mitchum by Reynolds. The newspapers had a field day. Mitchum went on to a glittering Hollywood career. He only played a boxer once in any of his subsequent films, portraying a faded heavyweight touring South America in *Second Chance*. The villain of the piece was played by Jack Palance, a genuine former professional heavyweight who had once gone the distance with contender Joe Baksi.

Bernie Reynolds's fighting career, which had once boasted a string of over twenty consecutive wins, never really took off. The year after the brawl in the Red Fox Bar, he was knocked out in two rounds in Cincinnati by the ex-world heavyweight title holder Ezzard Charles.

Perhaps Mitchum had softened him up.

177

# Brotherly Love

## Portland, Maine, March 1952

Rocky Marciano was one of the greatest of all world heavyweight champions. Rugged, durable and courageous, he retired undefeated after forty-nine contests, winning forty-three of these by knockouts. He was what was euphemistically referred to as a whole-hearted fighter. With Rocky anything went; butting, thumbing, hitting after the bell, holding with one hand and punching with the other, it was all part of the rich tapestry of life to the Rock. Every time that the Brockton Blockbuster left his corner he went winging out into a Pier Six brawl. Most of his opponents were less enthusiastic about the experience.

In the course of his ring career Rocky Marciano earned more than $3 million. Notoriously he was a careful man with money, secreting vast amounts in hiding places all over the USA. After one of his contests he was found placing his entire purse, over $40,000 in cash, in the water tank of the toilet in his hotel room. At the time of his premature death in a plane crash in 1969, it was estimated that the former champion had hidden hundreds of thousands of dollars in bank accounts under assumed names. None of it was ever recovered.

In his early days, Marciano's reluctance to spend money led to his being suspended for thirty days by the Maine Boxing Commission.

It started soon after the rising young heavyweight had announced his arrival on the big-time boxing scene by

178

knocking out former champion Joe Louis in eight rounds. He followed this by stopping another contender, veteran Lee Savold.

While Marciano was waiting for the current world champion, Jersey Joe Walcott, to defend his title against him, the Brockton fighter decided to cash in on his new-found fame by embarking upon a series of exhibitions around the state of Maine. Unfortunately the amateurs whom Rocky had hoped to persuade to travel with him as sparring partners and opponents had more sense than to agree to have their heads knocked off for nothing.

That left the young heavyweight in a quandary. The venues for the exhibitions had been booked and seats sold. More importantly, Marciano had been paid in advance. The prospect of handing back dollar bills was anathema to the future champion. So was the prospect of disgorging greenbacks and taking on professional sparring partners.

Rocky had an idea. He had a younger brother who was quite useful with the gloves; why not take him on in the place of hired help? The fact that Sonny Marciano was still at high school and weighed some thirty pounds less than his professional boxer brother could be discounted. After all, what was family for?

Not unnaturally, Sonny Marciano was less enamoured of the proposal, but not many people said no to Rocky, then or later. He agreed to accompany his brother on the tour, boxing in different towns under the names of Pete Fuller and Tony Zullo. The fact that Fuller was a leading amateur, a student at Harvard and a son of a former governor of Massachusetts, and was thus likely to be known by some of the spectators on their whistle-stop tour, did not seem to occur to the Marciano brothers.

The first contest on the tour went reasonably well. It took place in Lewiston. The eighteen-year-old Sonny was nervous at first, but although Rocky bustled in hard, the professional had the sense to pull most of his punches. Their bout was well received and the small circus went on to the next town in high spirits; this was like a licence to print money.

The tour proceeded and Sonny Marciano got more and more confident. It was a recipe for disaster. In the third of their bouts, at Portland, the younger brother decided that this professional boxing business was a doddle. Accordingly, after one brisk exchange of punches, instead of going back on the retreat as usual, Sonny Marciano sailed forward and hit his elder brother full on the jaw.

As soon as he had done so, Sonny knew that he had made a mistake. The blow was hard enough to knock Rocky Marciano's gum-shield out of his mouth. The heavyweight's eyes hardened and he moved forward meaningfully.

Sonny knew that he had committed more than a social error, he had put his life in danger. Desperately he scrambled backwards as his brother hurtled towards him.

'It's me!' screamed the high school student. 'I'm your brother! Don't hit me!'

To Sonny's indescribable relief, the words penetrated the red mist before Rocky Marciano's eyes. Reluctantly the heavyweight moved backwards and sparred gently for the rest of the round.

Sonny Marciano's life had been spared but the game was up. Most of the ringside spectators had heard the so-called Pete Fuller of Harvard screaming that he was Rocky Marciano's brother and begging Rocky to ease up.

Somebody reported the matter to the local commission. Rocky Marciano and the promoters of the bouts were given suspensions. Sonny Marciano lost his amateur status, even though he had received no payment for the bouts. Later he was reinstated.

Rocky Marciano went on to win the world title. He did not abandon his frugal ways. He met his death when he accepted a lift in a private aircraft, instead of taking a scheduled airline flight and buying a ticket.

# Heat Wave

## New York, June 1952

Between them Joey Maxim and Sugar Ray Robinson lost more than twenty pounds in weight during their contest for the former's world light heavyweight title, conducted in a heat wave in New York in 1952.

The temperature was over 80 degrees in the Yankee Stadium. Robinson, the world middleweight champion and former undefeated welterweight title holder, was considered to have a good chance against his bigger and slower opponent.

But that was reckoning without the heat. It was so enervating that both men were soon fighting in a pool of sweat.

The referee, Ruby Goldstein, was the first to go. At the end of the tenth round he staggered to the ropes and croaked that he could not carry on.

He was replaced by a substitute official, Ray Miller. Robinson made one last effort to finish Maxim off inside the distance. The stronger man weathered the storm. In the thirteenth round the middleweight champion put everything he had into one desperate last right hand. It missed and Robinson slumped to the canvas. He staggered up as the bell went. Robinson reeled about the ring, looking for his corner. His seconds came out and gently guided him back. They retired Robinson from the contest, stopped by the heat.

The middleweight received a great deal of sympathy for losing in such a fashion. It was estimated that by the time the bout was stopped the temperature had soared to well over 100 degrees.

The champion, Joey Maxim, was less sympathetic. 'So Robinson fought in a heat wave,' he said. 'Do you think my corner was air-conditioned?'

# A Man Could Get Killed!

## Helsinki, August 1952

When Ingemar Johansson, the Swedish heavyweight, entered the ring to fight in the final of the Olympic Games competition at Helsinki in 1952, the nineteen-year-old was a national hero. A few minutes later his name was mud. The boxer was accused in his nation's press of being a coward, a rat, a disgrace to his country and someone who should never be allowed to enter the ring again.

The gigantic Swede had been disqualified for not trying hard enough against his American opponent Ed Sanders.

Johansson had won his first three contests in the tournament on points and was considered to have quite a good chance against his opponent. Both the Swede and Sanders had hard punches, but each was a cautious fighter who preferred to let his opponent do the leading and then counter-punch.

Before the bout Johansson and his trainer decided that the Swede's course would be to retain his usual style and try to lure the American into making mistakes. Johannson admitted that he was nervous when he entered the ring for the final, and that it did occur to him that at this level of heavyweight boxing a man could get killed.

When the bell sounded to start the round, both boxers advanced carefully towards each other. Johansson stood stock still. Sanders weaved from side to side. Neither man struck a blow in the first round. Before they went back to their corners at the bell, the referee, Frenchman Roger Vaisberg, told both men that he wanted to see more action. So did the crowd, which was whistling derisively.

If the first round had been static, the second was comatose. Sanders and Johansson stood toe to toe without moving and without delivering a blow. Towards the end of the round the referee warned Johansson but not Sanders. The hall was in an uproar as the spectators demanded some sort of action.

The second round ended. Vaisberg walked over to Sanders's corner and lifted the American's hand. The Swede had been disqualified for not fighting.

Policemen had to escort Johansson from the ring and protect him from the abuse of the audience. He was not given the runner up's silver medal and at the presentation ceremony the Swedish flag was not unfurled.

Johansson never fought as an amateur again. He turned professional, surprised many by winning the European heavyweight title and then was matched against Floyd Patterson for the world championship.

Patterson had been one of the heroes of the Helsinki Olympics. While Johansson had been disqualified for lack of effort, Patterson had won the middleweight title in good style. He went on to win the world championship as a professional heavyweight, the youngest man until then to have done so.

Patterson was the 4-1 favourite to defeat the Swede, but in the third round he walked into a fusillade of punches and was stopped. Ingemar Johansson, the flop of Helsinki, was the world champion.

He lost his title to Patterson in a return fight and was knocked out in the sixth round in a third contest. But he had had his moment of glory.

As for Ed Sanders, the victor over Johansson in the Olympic final, he too turned professional and had a dozen fights. He died after the last one.

Ingemar Johansson's odd premonition before his bout with Ed Sanders that a man could get killed in the ring was realized in a dramatic and tragic fashion.

# *Room at the Top*

## Seattle, August 1957

Peter Rademacher was a career soldier, an officer in the US Army. He was also an outstanding amateur boxer. The balding, hard-punching Rademacher had been Northwest Golden Gloves champion four times, and was the Army and Inter-services heavyweight title holder.

The highlight of his amateur career came when Rademacher reached the final of the 1956 Melbourne Olympics and faced the Russian champion, Lev Moukhine. The American knocked his skilful opponent down for a count of eight and then swarmed all over Moukhine, until the referee stopped the fight in the first round.

Everyone thought that Rademacher would retire from the ring and concentrate on his Army career. After all, he was twenty-eight years old, and with the cachet of an Olympic gold medal to his credit he could go far in the military.

It was then that Rademacher announced that he was resigning his commission, leaving the army and fighting Floyd Patterson for the world professional championship at heavyweight.

At first Rademacher was thought to be joking. At his age he was far too old to embark upon a professional career, and no one could fight for the world championship in his first paid fight.

They were reckoning without Cus D'Amato. D'Amato was the manager of Floyd Patterson. An acerbic, volatile man, he was conducting a feud with the International Boxing Club which staged most major bouts in the USA. This meant that many of the leading heavyweights, who were tied to the IBC, could not meet the champion.

In addition, the shrewd manager realized that Patterson at 180 pounds was too light to go in with the really big heavyweights, and that his chin was suspect. What D'Amato had to do was to find his champion a series of bouts which looked reasonable on paper but which would not harm his protégé.

Rademacher was an ideal candidate. Big and with the prestige of being the current Olympic title holder, he was still no more than an amateur and could not possibly pull off an upset. Or so Cus D'Amato reckoned.

The ballyhoo started as the promoters tried to persuade the public that this was a fight worth watching. They were only partially successful. The box office gross was $243,000. Patterson took $250,000 as his share, which left the promoters and Rademacher scrambling for their cut from the television and ancillary rights. The challenger would probably have done better staying in the Army.

For a moment, however, he must have thought that destiny was on his side. He caught Patterson on the jaw with one of his powerful swings and sent the champion of the world to the canvas. Then Patterson got up and hammered the former amateur. The end came in the sixth round. Rademacher was knocked down for a count of eight with a right cross. The challenger got up, but was then floored with a volley of blows to the body. He did not beat the count.

Afterwards, Jack Hurley, a boxing manager who helped try to sell the ill-fated Patterson–Rademacher match to the public, shook his head sadly.

'It's a wonder the lot of us weren't thrown in gaol,' he said wonderingly.

# *All in the Family*

## Porthcawl, August 1960

The Londons were a well-known boxing family. They originated in West Hartlepool. Father Jack had won almost a hundred contests in a career extending over the 1930s and 1940s, and had held the British heavyweight title for a short period. His son Jack was a useful light heavyweight in the post-war years.

Perhaps the most successful of the London clan, however, was Jack's other son, Brian. Pugnacious, jutting-chinned and quick to react, as an amateur he won both the ABA and Empire Games heavyweight titles. As a professional he won the British championship and twice challenged unsuccessfully for the world crown.

It was generally admitted that Brian London had a fiery temperament and that some opponents tried to take advantage of this. One of his ring adversaries was the quick-witted Johnny Prescott, who defeated London towards the end of the latter's career in 1964. Prescott almost precipitated a brawl as he left the Liverpool arena after the bout and saw London signing autographs for a group of fans.

'Hey, Brian!' called Prescott cheerfully. 'You're not signing my name, are you?'

On that occasion Brian managed to restrain himself, but this was not always the case. At the celebrated Battle of Porthcawl, all three Londons found themselves heavily involved.

The Welsh resort was the scene of a contest between Brian

London and Dick Richardson for the latter's European heavyweight title. The bout took place in an open-air arena. For eight rounds London and Richardson hit each other with considerable enthusiasm but little finesse. Richardson was every bit as tough and hard-bitten as his challenger, so no quarter was given.

In the eighth round, Richardson opened an old cut over London's eye. The referee examined the gash and then stopped the bout in Richardson's favour.

Father Jack and brother Jack were incensed by the stoppage and decided that it was all Richardson's fault. This was a slightly obvious conclusion as the champion had been doing his best to inflict considerable bodily harm on Brian London all evening.

In any event, father Jack and brother Jack walked across the ring for a free and frank exchange of views with Dick Richardson and his handlers. With touching familial piety Brian went over with them.

The first inclination that Richardson's backers had that all was not well was when they looked up from their jubilant congratulations to see the three Londons looming over them. Richardson's trainer broke the silence.

'You're not going to effing well start again are you?' he asked plaintively.

He proved a true prophet. A large fist sent the trainer crashing to the canvas. In a moment almost everyone seemed to be engaged in the mayhem as punches flew wildly and bodies hit the floor.

The sight of the brawl was too much for many of the Welshmen in the audience. Dozens of them poured into the ring and started slugging it out indiscriminately with one another.

It was some considerable time before order could be restored. When the dust had finally settled it was agreed that Brian London's father and brother had been the principal instigators of the free-for-all, but the Board of Control fined Brian London £1000 for the disturbance. The boxer was also suspended for three months.

As a rider to their findings, the Board congratulated London's opponent Dick Richardson for his restraint and self-control during the mass punch-up. This must have gratified the European champion, who had once been described by his old opponent and Aldershot Army companion Henry Cooper as being 'as good a fighter on the cobbles as he was in the ring!'

# Famous Last Words

## New York, March 1965

Willie Pastrano was a beautiful boxer, light on his feet, intelligent and with a great left jab. He was also a witty and engagingly direct character.

He defended his world light heavyweight championship against Jose Torres and took a considerable beating. In the ninth round the champion was sent stumbling into the ropes after a vicious punch to the body. Pastrano's face was cut and bruised and he was gasping for breath.

The referee moved in to see if the champion was in a fit state to continue. He asked the stricken boxer the usual questions: who was he and where was he? Pastrano answered both questions satisfactorily. To make absolutely certain that the champion was in full possession of his senses, the referee persisted.

'What's happening to you?' he asked anxiously.

Pastrano's rueful answer has gone down in ring history.

'I'm getting the shit kicked out of me,' he replied.

The bout was stopped in the ninth round.

# The Invisible Punch

## Lewiston, Maine, May 1965

It is not often that the spectators at a world heavyweight title fight surround the ring at the end of the bout shouting 'Fake!' and 'Fix!', but that certainly happened after the bout between Cassius Clay, as he was then known, and Sonny Liston.

It was the second time that they had met. The year before, in February 1964, Clay had taken the championship from ex-gaolbird Liston in suspicious circumstances. The bout had ended with the supposedly invincible Liston sitting sullenly in his corner, claiming that he could not go on because he had hurt his shoulder. Liston had been the 8-1 favourite in the betting to retain his championship.

After the fiasco of the first bout, no major city would sanction holding the return match. In the end it was held in the small Maine township of Lewiston. Fewer than 3000 spectators turned up to watch the fight.

Those who did were rewarded by the spectacle of about fifty seconds of ineffectual sparring before Clay flicked out an innocuous-looking right hand to his opponent's head. Liston seemed to collapse in segments and then roll over on to his face.

The referee was Jersey Joe Walcott, a former heavyweight champion. He spent a few seconds trying to persuade Clay to retire to a neutral corner. The champion would not move at first but stood over the stricken Liston, gesturing to him to get up.

Finally Walcott began to count. Because of his altercation with Clay, he seemed to have lost touch with the count of the official timekeeper. Liston got up at the count of nine, but, by most reckonings, after he had been on the canvas for some fourteen seconds. The two men began sparring again.

At this stage Nat Fleischer, the diminutive seventy-five-year-old editor of the influential *Ring* magazine, took a hand. Fleischer was sitting at the ringside but had no official position at all. The veteran editor stood up, semaphoring his arms and ordering the referee to stop the fight.

For some reason Jersey Joe Walcott obeyed Fleischer. He moved in between Clay and Liston and raised the former's arm as the victor.

The way in which the contest had been halted and the disputed, or 'invisible' blow which had floored the champion inflamed the spectators. Clay later claimed that the knockout punch had been a perfect right cross delivered too fast for the layman's eye to witness. Most onlookers said that it had been a pathetic, limp delivery which would not have knocked the skin off a rice pudding.

Police had to hold members of the crowd back as they tried to storm the ring and get at both contestants. Liston ignored the noise. Clay shouted 'Shut-up!' at the spectators.

After the Lewiston disaster, politicians tried to introduce a bill into Congress to ban professional boxing. The state boxing commission held an enquiry into the events surrounding the contest and exonerated everyone. All the same, it was a long time before Sonny Liston could get a fight in the USA again. He had to go into exile in Sweden, winning a number of bouts there. Later he made a low-key comeback in the USA, rattling off a string of victories against second-rate fighters before falling to Leotis Martin. A year later he was found dead in his home, apparently from an overdose of drugs. Whether this was self-administered or whether the former champion had been murdered by gangland associates has never been made clear.

Cassius Clay became a member of the Black Muslim sect, changed his name to Muhammad Ali and went on to become one of the most popular and charismatic of heavyweight champions.

# Mexican Hayride

## Mexico City, October 1966

Billy Conn, the flamboyant and happy-go-lucky Irish American, was no stranger to controversy in or out of the ring. Once he had outboxed world heavyweight champion Joe Louis for thirteen rounds of their bout, only to get careless and walk into Louis's potent right hand. Afterwards Conn had chided the champion for his lack of consideration. If only Louis had consented to have been outpointed, said the challenger, he, Conn, could have kept the title for six lucrative months and then lost it back to Louis in a return contest. Louis had eyed the Irishman unblinkingly.

'How you going to hold the title six months when you couldn't even hold it thirteen rounds?' he had asked with deadly logic.

Conn had his share of trouble outside the ropes as well. At a domestic party, Mrs Conn's father, a former ball-player, delivered himself of one or two trenchant remarks about his daughter's choice of a husband. The ever-willing Conn had jumped up and challenged his father-in-law to settle their differences man to man. It being an Irish party, everyone present joined in. In the course of the ensuing scuffle, Conn, the only professional fighter present, suffered a broken bone in one hand.

Inevitably news of the brawl reached Joe Louis. Whenever he met Conn subsequently he would always enquire gravely, 'That father-in-law of yours still beating the hell out of you?'

It was no sinecure being related to Billy Conn. In his hotel room, while he was resting on the afternoon of the Joe Louis fight, he sprayed his sleeping brother with a seltzer bottle. In a moment the two Conns were fighting furiously. On another occasion, Billy Conn became involved in a restaurant brawl. Conn's brother-in-law came running to his assistance, only to walk into a wild right hand from the former light heavyweight champion.

However, the biggest altercation in Conn's life was not really his fault at all. It happened in Mexico City in 1966, when the ex-boxer was refereeing a lightweight contest between Sugar Ramos, a Mexican-domiciled Cuban, and Carlos Ortiz, a Puerto Rican living in New York.

The fight was held in the El Torea bull ring before 35,000 people, most of them rooting for Ramos. In the fifth round Conn stopped the fight because the Cuban had a badly gashed left eye. He awarded the verdict to Ortiz on a technical knockout.

There was a riot in the bull ring. Bottles and coins were hurled and Ortiz and Conn were hustled to the dressing-rooms in a wedge of policemen. The disturbances in the arena continued for several hours. The fans were only placated when Ramon Velazquez, secretary of the World Boxing Council, reversed the decision. He said that Ortiz had lost because he had refused to return to the ring to continue the fight with Ramos.

This did not please boxing supporters with Puerto Rican sympathies. Two thousand of them stormed a Bronx theatre where Mexican performers were appearing.

The other major boxing authority, the World Boxing Association, declared that it was quite impossible to reverse a referee's decision and that Ortiz was still the winner.

Conn had only one statement to make. In a television interview after his return to the USA, he was asked whether he would consider returning to Mexico for a holiday.

'I wouldn't fly over the place at a hundred thousand feet,' said the ex-champion tersely.

# No Contest!

## Rome, October 1968

No one ever got to the bottom of the unusual decision handed out in the Fred Little–Sandro Mazzinghi contest in Rome in 1968. The bout was for the Italian's world light middleweight title.

Little was on top of the contest from the start and at the end of the eighth round Mazzinghi went back to his corner bleeding badly from a number of cuts on his face. The doctor in attendance examined the cuts and told the referee that the Italian was in no state to continue.

The MC went to the centre of the ring and announced that Little was the winner and the new champion. It had seemed a fair result and there were no complaints from the home crowd.

Then the MC was summoned by the referee, who spoke to him urgently. Rather reluctantly, the MC returned to the centre of the ring and made another announcement. This time he declared that the referee had changed his decision. The bout had been declared 'no contest!'

Even the partisan Italian spectators could not stomach this verdict. They demonstrated loudly, throwing chairs and other missiles into the ring while the referee and both fighters beat a hasty retreat to safety.

Much later the referee attempted to give a reason for his sudden change of heart. He declared that there was a European Boxing Union rule that if a contest was stopped in the first half of a fight then it should be declared no contest.

Somewhat mysteriously the official went on to say that as far as he was concerned the interval between the eighth and ninth rounds constituted the first half of a fifteen-round bout.

The World Boxing Association, which was controlling the contest, received so many complaints about the strange circumstances surrounding the title fight that eventually they declared the title to be vacant. The board ordered the two men to fight again for the championship.

They never did, but justice of a sort was done a few months later when Fred Little fought Stan Hayward instead for the vacant title and won on points.

# Meeting of the Giants

## Miami, August 1969

Over the years there have been many heated discussions in bars and gyms as to the possible outcome of bouts between great fighters of different eras. Would John L Sullivan have lasted against Jack Dempsey? Could Gene Tunney have outsmarted Joe Louis? The permutations are endless.

In the summer of 1969, Murry Woroner, a Miami entrepreneur, did his best for the cause of legends by matching two of the greatest of all heavyweight champions, Rocky Marciano and Muhammad Ali.

It should have been a fight made in heaven, but there were a few minor clauses. For one thing, Marciano was forty-five years old and sixty pounds over his fighting weight. Ali was only twenty-five, but two years earlier had been stripped of his title and banned from boxing for refusing to serve in the US Army.

However, promoter Woroner had no intention of pitting the two men against each other in a genuine contest. He had conceived the bright idea of arranging a computerized fight between the two enormously popular heavyweights.

According to Woroner, every move and every blow ever struck by each fighter would be fed into a computer and from this a step-by-step account of the likely outcome of a bout between the two men would emerge. This print-out would be translated into a script and Marciano and Ali would enact the fight before television cameras.

Marciano came the cheaper of the two men at $10,000. Ali received one dollar short of $100,000. Both men had to work hard to get into shape for the fight. Ali had not been in the ring for two years, while Marciano had fought his last bout thirteen years before. The two men did their best in the time available, but despite all the efforts of the director and cameramen it is apparent in the film of their meeting that each man was still seriously overweight.

The bout was rehearsed in a small gymnasium at Miami Beach. The conditions were appalling. The gym was small, dirty and claustrophobic. There were no spectators, just the technicians and director. The two fighters worked eight hours a day, fighting one-minute rounds and then resting.

For both men it must have been a traumatic period. The white boxer's days of glory were over. Now he was just another former fighter. As far as Ali was concerned, his ring career might have been ended as well. He had offended the White Establishment.

The two fighters spent long periods talking together between takes and after the shooting. Both were sour and embittered men, suspicious of hangers-on. In his autobiography, Ali wrote of their growing friendship as fighters in a phoney world.

Altogether seven different endings were filmed for the bout. Neither boxer was supposed to know which one would be used in the final cut of the film; but both men realized that with the current state of Ali's unpopularity it was unlikely he would be shown defeating the former white heavyweight champion.

Only simulated punches were thrown in the filming. The sound effects were added later, together with a dubbed commentary and the shouts of an unseen crowd. The only time that there was any unpleasantness was when Ali inadvertently dislodged Marciano's treasured hairpiece.

When the film finally appeared, it was a financial success but a critical flop. Both men were obviously out of condition and far from their fighting best. It was shown simultaneously in 850 venues in the USA and another 500 around the world, grossing over two million dollars. In an extremely unconvincing bout Marciano was seen knocking Ali out in the thirteenth round.

Before it was shown, Ali had a change of heart and denounced the whole set-up on television. For this he was sued by the promoter. Rocky Marciano never lived to see the film. Before it was due to be released, at the beginning of 1970, he had died in an air crash.

# Return Fight Clause

## New York, January 1970

Ancient Archie Moore was one of the legends of the ring. His fighting career spanned twenty-six years and 234 contests, 199 of which he won. A succession of world champions carefully avoided getting into the ring with him, and he was thirty-six years old before he outpointed Joey Maxim for the light heavyweight championship. At the age of thirty-nine he was still good enough to put Rocky Marciano on the canvas in their bout for the heavyweight title, before his legs gave out and he was forced to give up in the ninth round.

George Plimpton, on the other hand, was a writer and a very good one. He founded the literary magazine *Paris Review* and then began to make a speciality of writing about sport from the inside. His pre-season training spell with the Detroit Lions provided the material for one of the best books on sport ever written, *Paper Lion*. He also talked himself into pitching for a major league baseball team at the Yankee Stadium, an episode which saw print in another enthralling book, *Out of My League*.

These had been fascinating experiences, extremely well described, but when Plimpton told his friends that his next exploit would be to box three rounds against Archie Moore at Stillman's gym in New York, they reckoned that this time he had gone too far.

Plimpton's friends did their best to dissuade him. One of them sent him, anonymously, a series of notes describing the reactions of famous boxers to the beatings they had taken. These included Max Baer's famous dictum:

'If you get belted and see three fighters through a haze, go after the one in the middle. That's what ruined me – going after the other two guys.'

Plimpton prepared for the contest in his own idiosyncratic way. He read a few old books on boxing in the library of the Racquet Club in New York, and in order to get the feel of the professional ring he attended a weighing-in ceremony at the New York Boxing Commission's headquarters for a professional tournament taking place that evening. Plimpton had intended stripping off and weighing in with the others, but when he saw the onlookers regarding his stick-insect-like form with incredulity, he abandoned the idea.

There was a precedent for such an encounter. Back in the 1920s, the famous writer Paul Gallico, who later published *The Snow Goose*, was a young sports writer. He allowed himself to be persuaded by his editor to enter the ring with Jack Dempsey, then preparing for a contest. The idea was that Gallico would write a piece about what it was like to face the mighty champion in a sparring bout.

Unfortunately some evil-minded person whispered to Dempsey that the well-built but peaceful Gallico was in reality an up-and-coming young fighter from Canada determined to gain a reputation at Dempsey's expense. Dempsey flattened Gallico with his opening punch.

Archie Moore was a little more generous to George Plimpton. He gave the young writer a fairly torrid opening round, but when he realized the ineptitude of his adversary, he eased up considerably until the end of the sparring bout.

All the same, Plimpton had taken some hard shots to the body. He could hardly move after the contest. Some time later he was still sitting in the dressing-room being sick into a bucket, when Archie Moore came in to bid him farewell.

The former champion eyed the hapless Plimpton with a glint in his eye and then murmured gravely:

'Remember, George, you're entitled to a rematch!'

# Rocky!

Towards the end of 1974, the charismatic Muhammad Ali had made boxing history by regaining his world heavyweight championship after knocking out George Foreman in eight rounds. Ali had confounded the experts with his 'rope-a-dope' technique of leaning on the ropes and allowing the cumbersome champion to punch himself out before Ali moved in for the kill.

For his first defence of his new crown, Ali looked round for someone who would not give him much more than an extended workout. He would soon be fighting his old opponent Joe Frazier again, and that should be a war. At the beginning of 1975, a less fearsome adversary was required.

The fighter selected was Chuck Wepner, a white heavyweight from Bayonne, New Jersey. Wepner had been a professional for eleven years, starting his career with a knockout win over George Cooper in Bayonne, in 1964. Since then he had taken part in forty-one bouts. He had gone in with Buster Mathis, Joe Bugner, George Foreman, Jerry Tomasetti and Bob Stallings. The trouble was they had all beaten him, most of them inside the distance.

Chuck's main drawback was that he suffered badly from facial cuts. He usually ended a bout looking like Kirk Douglas in one of the latter's more masochistic roles. So renowned did Wepner become for his tendency to cut up that he became known as the 'Bayonne Bleeder'.

Still, the heavyweight was brave and willing, and at 6 feet 5 inches and 250 pounds he looked the part of a contender. Wepner grabbed the chance to appear in a nationally televised bout for the world title at a time when he must have been considering retiring. He prepared to sell his life dearly.

Ali danced around Wepner for the first eight rounds, peppering the slow-moving challenger with rapid lefts. It looked like being another easy points win for the champion and a suitable way to get into shape for the forthcoming bout with Frazier.

In the ninth round things went slightly awry for the champion. Ali was still dancing like a butterfly, but at one stage he moved in a little too close to his big-hitting challenger. Wepner seized the opportunity and knocked Ali down with a scything right to the body.

The champion scrambled to his feet at once, claiming hotly that he had been tripped, but was forced to suffer the indignity of a standing count of eight.

Wepner did his best to capitalize on his lusty right hand punch, but his moment of glory was almost over. Ali did not give the Bayonne Bleeder another chance. By the fifteenth round Wepner was exhausted. Ali knocked him out with only nineteen seconds of the round and the contest to go.

It was the end of the road for Wepner and just another fight for the champion. Yet the Ali–Wepner bout was to give birth to a show-business phenomenon – the *Rocky* movies.

One of the millions of viewers who saw Wepner unexpectedly floor Muhammad Ali in their Cleveland bout was an unsuccessful small-part film actor and would-be writer called Sylvester Stallone. Stallone had played small parts in such films as *The Prisoner of Second Avenue* and *Farewell My Lovely* as a hoodlum, but at the age of thirty was beginning to wonder if he was going to make it.

After seeing the Ali–Wepner contest, he spent four days writing a script about an unsuccessful heavyweight who gets a chance to fight for the heavyweight championship. Although given no chance, the fighter manages to secure a draw, and a return fight. This led the way to a sequel and then a number of others.

At first Stallone had no luck with his script, but then managed to interest producer Irwin Winkler. Winkler was impressed and offered the young writer $300,000 for the rights. Stallone was broke, with a pregnant wife, but refused the offer. Winkler could have the script for $75,000 and a percentage of the profits, offered the writer, but he, Stallone, had to play the lead.

Winkler took a chance on the unknown and *Rocky* was made, starring Sylvester Stallone and directed by John G Avildsen. It proved to be the most successful film at the box-office for twenty years. It won Oscars for best film, best director and best editing.

The climax of the film is the fight for the title between Rocky and Apollo Creed, the champion, played by Carl Weathers, once with the Oakland Raiders. Stallone claimed to have choreographed the contest on the first bout between Rocky Marciano and Ezzard Charles.

*Rocky* was so successful and profitable that it spawned no fewer than four sequels, *Rocky II*, *Rocky III*, *Rocky IV* and *Rocky V*.

# A Matter of Record

## Florida, February 1977

Scott LeDoux was a useful American heavyweight who had boxed draws with two leading fighters, Ken Norton and Leon Spinks, and gone in with most other top Americans. Later he was to challenge Larry Holmes for one version of the heavyweight title, lasting seven rounds. A schoolteacher outside the ring, LeDoux had a highly developed sense of justice. It was to be outraged in his contest with Johnny Boudreaux in Florida.

The bout was part of a tournament organized by promoter Don King and backed by ABC television to find the US heavyweight champion. Similar tournaments were being held in the other weight divisions.

The idea was that such a series of elimination contests would unify all the different bodies with their so-called champions. The smooth-talking King, who had served a four year prison sentence for manslaughter, persuaded the television executives that everything would be above board because the fighters selected for the tournaments would be chosen as a result of their ring records, verified by the trusted *Ring* magazine. This was enough to persuade ABC to pay Don King $2 million.

The tournament started by being chaotic and rapidly got worse. *Ring* magazine was supposed to select the best dozen boxers in most of the weight divisions, and these twelve fighters would become involved in a series of elimination contests to find the US champion in each class.

Somehow a number of the most inept fighters in the USA suddenly found themselves rated in the top twelve in their weight class. Their only qualifications seemed to be that they were well-connected – usually with Don King.

Boxers were included in the tournament who had never fought in the particular weight division in which they were included, one had lost seventeen of his last nineteen bouts, and one was said to have lost a total of seventy contests in the course of his ring career.

Before the tournaments had even got under way they had already lost all credibility with the sporting press. Shrewd reporters began to dig into the records produced by their managers and supported by *Ring* magazine, and discovered dozens of errors. Honest managers found that they had to part with money before their fighters could be included in the eliminators.

The LeDoux–Boudreaux contest caused so much controversy that the television company withdrew its support and the whole idea withered on the vine, although the irrepressible Don King went on to consolidate his position as a major promoter.

LeDoux seemed to have coasted his way to an easy points victory. He knocked Boudreaux down early in the bout and kept on top of his adversary for the entire eight rounds. At the end of the fight the referee raised Boudreaux's hand in victory.

The crowd hooted the decision and Scott LeDoux stamped about the ring shouting, 'Fake!' At one point he even aimed a kick at his opponent. It missed and knocked off the toupee of Howard Cosell, the distinguished commentator sitting at ringside.

The shambles of the verdict and the unfortunate accident to Cosell was reported all over the USA. The ABC network hired a firm of lawyers to investigate the accusations of dishonesty. The enquiry revealed a sorry story of chicanery and opportunism on the part of the promoters.

Don King took it all in his stride. 'Boxing's a funny business,' he shrugged. 'Lot of liars about.'

# *Down but Not Out*

## Boston, February 1979

Sugar Ray Seales was the only member of the USA's boxing team to win a gold medal at the 1972 Olympics in Munich. He turned professional and was expected to become the middleweight champion of the world.

Seales did reasonably well at first, but there were one or two inexplicable losses on his record. The former Olympic champion did not seem to be living up to his potential.

It was generally accepted that Sugar Ray had a chance to put his faltering career back on the rails when he was matched to fight the up-and-coming Marvin Hagler in Boston. They had already fought twice. Hagler had won the first on points and they had drawn the second. The winner of the rubber contest could be expected to go on to a bout for the world title.

It was all over in a round. Hagler overwhelmed Seales and knocked him out with contemptuous ease. Later in the same year he boxed a draw with Vito Antuofermo for the world championship, and a year later knocked out Alan Minter in London for the title.

Seales boxed on for a little while, winning some and losing some, and then retired from the ring. When he did so he announced that for the last two years of his boxing life he had been totally blind in one eye and had severely impaired sight in the other.

Many of these fights had been in small halls in obscure parts of the country, but a number had been in major venues. When

208

asked how he had managed to pass the pre-fight medical examinations, the boxer shrugged and said that he had memorized the sight-charts and that in any case he had never been subjected to anything but the most perfunctory of checks.

Seales had undergone operations to repair detached retinas in both eyes. He claimed that in one of his last contests, against Max Hord in Denver, he had been almost blind but had connected with a lucky blow.

A number of entertainers, including Sammy Davis Junior, and boxing stars such as Muhammad Ali, rallied round Seales and appeared at a special benefit performance for the legally blind fighter at Tacoma. With Seales's luck, the show lost $20,000.

'I'm down but not out,' said Sugar Ray Seales afterwards.

# A Nice Little Earner

## Bloomington, August 1979

Heavyweights Ken Norton and Scott LeDoux put up a spirited ten-round contest at Bloomington, Minnesota, with the veteran Norton just squeezing the decision on points. Both contestants then left the ring to pick up their cheques from the promoter. They were splitting $265,000, with about $200,000 of this going to Norton. For the black heavyweight it was his best purse since the heady days when he had fought Muhammad Ali for the championship. It was the most money that LeDoux had ever earned in the ring.

Neither boxer realized it but they were taking part in one of the most amazing promotions ever witnessed in the USA. The tournament was one of a series put on by an entrepreneur new to the boxing world, a bearded black man who called himself Harold J Smith, which was not his real name.

Smith had promoted a few unsuccessful rock concerts but had no other experience of staging multi-million dollar extravaganzas when he burst upon the boxing scene. He declared that he had unlimited funds and that he was determined to become the number one boxing promoter in the USA.

For a time it looked as if Smith might do it. He managed to persuade the unwitting Muhammad Ali to lend his name to an organization which Smith called Muhammad Ali Professional Sports. Smith then proceeded to set up a series of boxing programmes across the USA, flying to each one in his executive jet, accompanied on the flight by a large group of associates, girlfriends and hangers-on.

At first the major promoters such as Don King and Bob Arum laughed at the newcomer with the big ideas. There was no way that Smith could muscle in, they declared. There was. Smith set up his promotions by the simple method of paying the boxers he used at least twice as much as they had ever received for a fight before.

It was not long before managers and their fighters were clamouring to be employed by the new force in professional boxing. King and Arum could not understand it. With the money he was paying, they declared, there was no way that Harold J Smith could be making a profit from his promotions.

In no way put off, Smith then announced plans for his greatest production yet, an $8 million dollar supershow at Madison Square Garden. The promoter announced some of the star fighters who would be appearing and the massive sums they would earn. Heavyweights Gerry Cooney and Ken Norton were to receive more than $1 million each. Middleweight Tommy Hearns would get $1½ million. Matthew Saad Muhammad would be paid $2 million. The show, appropriately enough, would be called 'This Is It!'

But it wasn't. Almost immediately the bubble burst. It turned out that Smith had been losing hundreds of thousands of dollars on his tournaments all over the country and his incredible life-style.

The money to launch the whole carnival had come from one of Smith's partners, who had embezzled $21 million dollars from the Wells Fargo National Bank where he worked. Smith and two others were put on trial and pleaded guilty to embezzling the cash. Smith was sent to prison for ten years, while his colleagues received lesser sentences.

Slowly boxing returned to normal. King and Arum went around smugly saying, 'I told you so!' But a lot of boxers had a little extra in their bank accounts to go with their cuts and bruises suffered in the service of Harold J Smith.

# 'No Mas!'

## New Orleans, November 1979

Roberto Duran of Panama was reputed to be one of the toughest fighters of his time, a *macho* contestant who never took a backward step. Brought up in the slums of the city, he was reputed to have knocked out grown men in street fights before he was even in his teens. There was even a story that he had once hit a horse and stunned it, although his mother always denied the canard, attributing it to an uncle from a less reputable branch of the family.

The snarling, aggressive Duran was a natural to become a professional fighter. In 1972 he won the world lightweight title by knocking out Ken Buchanan of Scotland. He defended it fourteen times. In 1980, he won the welterweight title by outpointing the highly regarded stylist, Sugar Ray Leonard.

Five months later the two men were matched again. To the amazement of the crowd, Duran fought an oddly subdued fight. In the eighth round, the champion suddenly dropped his hands and said, 'No mas!' ('No more!')

It was the most surprising capitulation in the ring of modern times. Afterwards Duran put the blame on stomach cramps, others said that he had taken off too much weight too quickly.

Whatever the cause, the *macho* man had quit.

# 'Nor Iron Bars a Cage ...'

## New Jersey, 1970–80

A number of boxers have served time in gaol. Among world champions, Sonny Liston spent several terms behind bars, while Jack Johnson boxed at Leavenworth and Rocky Graziano was on the boxing team in a military stockade. Of British champions, both Dick Burge and Pedlar Palmer served terms of imprisonment.

Rahway State Prison in the USA made a virtue of a necessity by including a boxing course as part of the rehabilitation programme for its inmates. Not only were prisoners encouraged to box, the project became so successful that a number of professional tournaments were held inside the prison and televised nationally.

Eleven boxing tournaments were held at Rahway, and more than half of them were seen on television. Visiting boxers would visit the gaol and fight the home boys.

The success of the tournament owed a lot to one particular inmate, a light heavyweight called James Scott. While he was at Rahway he defeated a number of highly ranked contenders in good style.

It was not long before the fighting convict had a national following. People thrilled to the prospect of an under-privileged member of society fighting his way to success. A glittering career was forecast for Scott after he had paid his debt to society and could concentrate on a full-time boxing career.

It was not to be. When Scott was released, he did take up professional boxing but lost a couple of bouts straight away. It was not long before he was back in Rahway. This time he did not apply for the boxing rehabilitation programme.

# Enough Is Enough

## Houston, November 1982

Randall 'Tex' Cobb was one of the wittiest and toughest of all heavyweight contenders. Even after the bloodiest contest he would still have a quip and a one-liner for the reporters. Yet one of his bouts was so one-sided and gory that the USA's leading boxing commentator swore he would never cover the fight game again.

Cobb was matched to fight the undefeated Larry Holmes for the WBC version of the world heavyweight title. The Texan approached the contest with his usual airy detachment. When asked what his price for the contest was, he said that he would be charging his customary fee of twenty-five cents and a loose woman. His game plan, he told reporters, would be as usual, 'stumbling forward and getting hit in the face!'

The truth turned out to be uncannily close to the fighter's lighthearted forecast. The judges were unanimous in their verdict that Holmes won fourteen of the fifteen rounds by large margins, and that one of the rounds was even.

Cobb refused to go down but shipped terrible punishment. Hardened observers among the press corps were screaming at the referee to stop the fight as Cobb soaked up blow after blow.

When the bout was over and the obvious verdict announced, Howard Cosell, who had described the contest for ABC television and was accepted as the country's leading sports commentator, said that he had been so disgusted by the mismatch and the way in which Cobb had been allowed to continue when he had no chance, that he would never again broadcast on professional boxing. 'I don't want to be a party to the sleaziness,' he shuddered.

As usual, Tex Cobb was phlegmatic. When asked if he had tried to talk to Holmes during their contest, he said, 'Every time I tried speaking to him I found it hard, because he kept putting his left hand in my mouth!'

# Like Father, Like Son

## Atlantic City, June 1983

Joe Bugner was one of the most exasperating of a long line of disappointing British heavyweight champions. On a number of occasions in the ring he flattered only to deceive. He had a great deal in his favour – strength, a good chin, courage, resilience and a fair punch. Yet he seemed to lack the will to succeed.

At his best, Bugner was on the fringes of world class. At his worst, he could be dire. And in a late attempt at a comeback, he engaged in a strange contest which somehow summarized the disparities of his long fighting career.

The Hungarian-born Bugner's best performance came while he was still in his early twenties, against the American heavyweight Joe Frazier. This bout took place in London in 1973.

Not long before, Frazier had been one of the most fearsome of all world heavyweight champions. Earlier that year he had lost his title to George Foreman. He had previously defeated Muhammad Ali and later was to engage in two more thrilling losing contests with the Louisville Lip. At this time, therefore, Frazier was far from being a spent force.

Yet the young and handsome Joe Bugner confounded his critics by putting up the fight of his life against the former champion. With incredible courage and enthusiasm, he fought toe-to-toe with the strong Frazier. Even when he was floored for a long count in the tenth round, Bugner climbed back to his feet and by the end of the twelfth he had his opponent rocking. Bugner lost the contest on points but it was to be his finest hour. Never again did he fight as well as he had against Joe Frazier.

There were to be many more contests, in venues as far apart as the USA, Copenhagen, Bologna, Kuala Lumpur and London, against such tough opponents as Muhammad Ali, Earnie Shavers and Ron Lyle, most of which he lost.

A decade later Bugner was still fighting, this time in Atlantic City. It would have been just another fight but for the opponent in the opposite corner. Bugner was matched against a Frazier again, only this time he was fighting Joe's son, Marvis.

This is one of the very few recorded instances of a boxer fighting a father and his son in the course of a career. There was to be no repeat of the heady success against Joe Frazier ten years earlier. The thirty-three-year-old Bugner was ten years older and, at almost 240 pounds, much heavier than he had been in his prime. He plodded to a dull ten-round defeat at the fists of his much lighter and younger opponent. Joe Frazier, long since retired from the ring, was in his son's corner for the bout. He saw his son advance constantly throughout the fight, while Bugner retreated and counter-punched, using all his accumulated experience to keep out of trouble.

After the points decision in favour of Marvis Frazier had been announced, Bugner went through the ritual of disputing the decision, but his heart did not seem to be in it.

Like his father, Marvis Frazier went on to challenge for the world heavyweight title, but he did not emulate Joe Frazier's success. Marvis was knocked out in the first round by Larry Holmes.

Bugner fought on for a few more years, settled in Australia and even secured several points wins over fair-class American heavyweights. He was crushed in a much-hyped bout in London against Frank Bruno, and announced his permament retirement from the ring.

# The Tampered Gloves

## New York, June 1983

One of the great clichés in boxing movies is the moment when the villain has something done to his gloves which gives him an unfair advantage over the hero and enables him to win the fight. A typical example is *City for Conquest*. James Cagney's opponent in a big fight is being beaten by the hero. The villain's seconds smear their man's gloves with grease. He uses this to pick up resin from the canvas and then rub it into Cagney's eyes, blinding him permanently.

Such plots are now derided as being far-fetched, but at Madison Square Garden in 1983, a young boxer was so badly beaten by unfair means that he never fought again.

The fight was the main supporting event to the contest in which Roberto Duran took the world light middleweight title from Davey Moore. The two contestants in the supporting bout were also light middleweights. Red-haired Billy Ray Collins Junior was an undefeated young prospect from Nashville, Tennessee, managed by his father, a former boxer. Collins was considered to be on his way up. The Madison Square Garden contest was supposed to be a showpiece for his talents.

Collins's opponent was Luis Resto, an undistinguished fighter with a poor record and a reputation for not being able to hit very hard.

To everyone's surprise, Resto swarmed all over Collins from the first round, punishing him savagely. Collins seemed totally unable to ward off his opponent and was staggered on a number of occasions.

Between rounds, Collins's father did his best to patch up his son. He was amazed and disturbed at the amount of facial bruising that Billy Junior seemed to be picking up. The young fighter was unable to account for the beating he was taking, but told his father that he felt as if he were being hit about the face and body with a stick.

Collins fought back manfully and the contest was an exciting one, but at the end of the ten rounds Luis Resto was declared an easy winner. Collins stumbled back to his corner. Both his eyes were closed and he looked, his father said, as if he had been mugged.

Billy Collins Senior left the other second to patch up his son. He walked across the ring to Resto's corner to congratulate the victor. Automatically he extended his hand to shake the other fighter's glove. As he did so, he sensed something wrong about the feel of the glove. Collins retained his grip and shouted to officials that he wanted the gloves impounded and checked.

The eight-ounce gloves were removed from the protesting Luis Resto and taken away for analysis. It was discovered that both gloves now weighed less than seven ounces. Close inspection revealed that there were microscopic slits in the padding of the gloves and that some of the stuffing had been surreptitiously removed. Resto had been hitting his opponent with hardly anything over his knuckles, which would explain the cuts and bruises on Billy Ray Collins's face.

A full investigation was carried out by the Boxing Commission. It transpired that the gloves had been delivered from the manufacturer by a representative of the promoter to another official at an hotel across the way from the stadium. The second official brought the gloves across to Madison Square Garden, where they were distributed to the fighters in the dressing-rooms. Somewhere along the way the padding had been removed.

The Commission banned Resto's trainer and second for life and placed an indefinite ban on their fighter. Later the trainer was sentenced to a term of three to six years in prison and Resto was sentenced to one to three years for assault and conspiracy. Resto was also charged with being in possession of a deadly weapon – his fighter's fists wrapped in tape.

Billy Ray Collins Junior never fought again. He started drinking heavily and left his wife. Less than a year after his dreadful beating at Madison Square Garden, his car went out of control and crashed into a creek. Billy Ray did not survive.

# The Long Round

Sun City, Bophuthatswana, December 1984

It was one of those days for South African heavyweight Gerrie Coetzee. He was defending his World Boxing Association version of the heavyweight championship against his American challenger Greg Page.

In the course of the contest's eight bizarre rounds, not a great deal went right for Coetzee. The South African was a ponderous fighter, chiefly famed for his so-called 'bionic' right hand. Actually, this designation referred not to the strength of the punch but to the fact that Coetzee had broken the hand six times and undergone fifteen operations on it.

In the contest at the Superbowl things began to go wrong for Coetzee quite early on. When the bell rang for the second round, the champion's seconds were slow to leave the ring. Coetzee turned to continue a casual conversation with his handlers, and was half sitting and half standing as they removed the stool.

Never one to waste an opportunity, Page promptly raced across and hit the South African hard on the head while the champion's back was still turned.

Coetzee was momentarily stunned but managed to turn and resume the contest. He fought back with some spirit and considerable indignation. At the end of the sixth round, however, he lumbered into trouble again. The bell rang and the champion trustingly lowered his hands. Happily Page hit him with a long left, knocking him to the canvas.

222

The South African's handlers screamed their protests at the referee, who warned the American heavyweight but did not deduct any points from his total.

The now discouraged Coetzee needed several rounds to recover from this latest unexpected blow and he took quite a hiding in the seventh, being floored again, this time legitimately.

By the eighth round the South African had begun to come back into the fight. Another minute's rest and he might even have started to trouble the challenger.

Unfortunately the champion was not to be granted the privilege of the customary rest period at the end of the three-minute round. The electronic clock timing the rounds malfunctioned and did not give the signal for the bell to be rung.

The two bewildered and exhausted heavyweights struggled on. Coetzee was the first to wilt. Page caught him with a left to the jaw. The champion crashed flat on his back and was counted out.

It was later discovered that the eighth round had lasted three minutes and fifty seconds, almost a minute over the limit.

The South African's backers were furious, but their appeals to have the verdict reversed or the bout declared no-contest were ignored.

'We're sick about everything,' said Coetzee's second, Willie Lock.

# The Rose Tattoo

## Norfolk, Virginia, July 1985

It was the greatest night of Roberto Medina's fighting life. A relative novice, with twelve wins, a loss and a draw on his record, he had been matched with former Olympic gold medallist Meldrick Taylor in a bout televised nationally by ABC.

Sporting his trademark, a rose tattoo on his chest, Medina piled in against the skilful Olympian and did his best to hustle Taylor out of his stride. Taylor was stung into action and responded with flurries of deadly punches.

Soon Medina was rocking from side to side beneath the onslaught of his opponent, but he refused to go down. Doggedly he fought back, although shipping considerable punishment.

For eight rounds the two lightweights put up an exciting if one-sided bout, with Taylor handing it out and Medina receiving. Every so often Medina would go in on a swing and a prayer and receive the plaudits of the excited crowd for his courage.

The decision in favour of Taylor was a foregone conclusion but the loser was cheered all the way back to his dressing-room for his display of heart. When he reached the changing area, however, he found a different kind of reception.

A dozen Norfolk policemen surrounded the dressing-room and moved in on Medina, arresting him on the spot. It transpired that the fighter was an escaped convict named John Garcia.

Garcia had escaped from an open prison in Colorado by the simple expedient of walking out through the gate after serving seven years of a sentence for robbery. He had a record of over sixty arrests for theft.

Garcia had been hidden by a cousin in St Petersburg, obtained employment as a handyman and even started going steady with a girl. In an effort to supplement his income, he had taken up professional boxing.

His gift for the sport had been his undoing. If Garcia had been content to remain a bottom-of-the-bill fighter he probably would never have been recognized. However, his run of victories had led to his appearing a number of times on cable television. A former girlfriend had seen one of his bouts and had given Garcia away to the authorities. She informed them that the rose tattoo on her former boyfriend's chest was a giveaway.

Alerted by the Norfolk police force, a number of officials who had known Garcia in his previous incarnation watched the bout with Taylor on national television. They were able to confirm that the fighter called Medina was in fact the escaped convict John E Garcia.

Garcia made no effort to escape when he was arrested in the dressing-room. 'He was kind of high because he had put up such a good fight,' said Lt Curtis Todd Jr of the Norfolk Police Department.

The warm glow resulting from going the distance with the Olympic gold medallist evidently did not wear off quickly. As Garcia was in the process of being transported back to prison, all he would say was, 'What a fight! We put on a helluva show for the fans!'

# A Difference of Opinion

## London, November 1985

The middleweight contest between Mark Kaylor and Errol Christie at Wembley was a cracker. The men were competing for a total purse of £82,000, the highest ever paid for a non-title bout in Great Britain.

Christie was knocked down in the first round but got up to floor Kaylor twice. Kaylor then came back and knocked his opponent out in the eighth round.

It was an excellent fight considering that at one time it had looked as if it would be cancelled. Only a few weeks before the contest, the two men at a press luncheon had traded the usual carefully rehearsed insults which are used to build up interest in a bout. The boxers must have put a little too much heart into their delivery, because before the assembled journalists could do anything about it, Taylor and Christie were swapping punches for real.

Eventually they were separated, but as a result of the adverse publicity, the local police were reluctant to see the bout go ahead. Kaylor was white and Christie black, and the authorities feared a race riot at Wembley when they met in the ring.

In the end the bout took place, but Kaylor was fined £15,000 by the Boxing Board of Control, while Christie was ordered to pay £5000. Both men appealed, and in the light of their subsequent good behaviour in the ring the sums were reduced.

# Double Header

## Atlantic City, August 1988

It must have seemed a good idea at the time. The holders of two different versions of the world welterweight title were to top the bill against carefully selected opponents in a double header. Each man would defend his piece of the title against a relatively easy opponent. The two champions were expected to win their bouts comfortably. Then, at a later date, they could be matched against each other in a lucrative unification contest.

Unfortunately, the two hapless challengers did not adhere to the script, thus causing the promoters considerable grief.

In the first contest, the acerbic British holder of the World Boxing Council title, Lloyd Honeyghan, was matched against the Korean contender Youngkil Chung.

Chung was not expected by the experts to last long, but he put up a surprisingly good showing. On several occasions he drove the champion back with fierce attacks. At the end of the third round Chung hit Honeyghan as the bell sounded. The champion hit his opponent back and received a warning for fighting after the bell.

At the start of the fifth round Honeyghan appeared to be getting on top. Then suddenly he threw a long left which hit Chung below the belt. The challenger hesitated and then fell to the canvas, clutching his groin and writhing like a landed fish.

The crowd jeered heartily. Chung's supporters accused

Honeyghan of foul fighting, while Honeyghan's followers declared that the Korean's reaction to the blow had been over-dramatic.

After the challenger had been writhing on the canvas for two or three minutes, Chung was hauled up on to a stool by his seconds. He sat slumped forward, insisting that he could not carry on.

Instead of disqualifying Honeyghan for the low blow, the referee declared, quite rightly, that if Chung was not capable of fighting on after a five-minute break, then the decision would be awarded to the champion. Chung refused to stand up. He was declared the loser on a technical knockout.

While the Koreans in the crowd were still protesting at the decision, the second welterweight championship bout was hastily got under way.

If the first bout had been an embarrassment for the promoters, the second was a disaster. It was between Marlon Starling, the World Boxing Association holder of the welterweight title, and Tomas Molinares, a relatively unknown challenger from Columbia.

Molinares got off to a good start but by the sixth round the hard-hitting Starling was beginning to forge ahead on the scorecards of all the officials.

The bell rang to end the round. Starling dropped his hands and started to turn to walk back to his corner. Molinares stepped forward and hit the champion on the jaw with a vicious right hand. Starling dropped unconscious to the canvas.

After the débâcle of the Honeyghan-Chung contest this latest breach of the rules almost sparked off a riot. When the spectators had run out of breath they stopped shouting and waited for the master of ceremonies to announce that Molinares had been disqualified.

Instead it was declared over the microphone that the blow had started before the bell had sounded and therefore was a legitimate one. Molinares was the winner and new champion by a knockout.

It had been obvious to everyone at the ringside that

Molinares had not even started the knockout punch when the bell had sounded, so the uproar began all over again.

When the smoke had cleared, the onlookers realized that one champion had retained his title by delivering a foul punch, and that the other had kept his because he had been knocked out by another rule-bending blow.

# Poor Losers

Tokyo, September 1964. Seoul, September 1988

The South Koreans have produced some splendid boxers who have gone on to win Olympic medals and professional championships. They have also provided several of the world's worst losers.

The first of these was Dong-Kih Cho, who represented his country at the 1964 Olympics, the first to be held in Asia. Unfortunately his total fighting time in the ring occupied less than three minutes, although he remained within the roped square for a much longer period.

The flyweight was disqualified in the first round for fighting on after the referee had ordered him to stop. It took some time for the loser to appreciate that his brief foray into Olympic boxing was over. When the realization sank in, Dong-Kih Choh was less than enamoured. He stormed about the ring, expostulated with his seconds, complained to the referee and appealed to his fellow countrymen in the audience. It was all in vain.

Then the disgruntled flyweight did what any self-respecting protester would do. He marched to the centre of the ring and lowered himself into a sitting position.

Dong-Kih Choh sat in the ring of the Olympic stadium for almost an hour, ignoring the hoots and whistles of the spectators hoping to see some more boxing. At first officials tried to reason with the boxer. Then they argued. They tried ordering him out of the ring. At one point they even tried to

230

manhandle him bodily through the ropes. The diminutive boxer put up such a struggle that they abandoned the idea and put him back.

Finally they tried bribery. The officials approached the sulking flyweight and promised him that if he left the ring and allowed the next pair of contestants to enter they would order a review of the referee's decision against him. Reluctantly Dong-Kih Choh left the ring and walked away into fistic obscurity, his fifty minutes of notoriety over.

But the memory lingered on. The South Korean boxers must have wondered if they could ever again hold up their heads in international competition. Time passed and the medals and titles started to accumulate once more. Just when it must have seemed safe to enter the ring with some confidence, the 1988 Olympics in Seoul came along.

The venue might have changed but the ambience remained much the same. In fact, the entire boxing competition in the Korean Games could have been said to have been star-crossed. The organization was less than streamlined. Two adjacent rings were in operation at the same time. Unfortunately, the bouts in the different rings were not synchronized. Boxers became confused between the bells. The bell would sound in one ring and a boxer in the other would drop his hands obediently and get tagged by a punch.

There was almost a riot when the American light middleweight Roy Jones comprehensively outboxed the South Korean Park Si-hun but was adjudged to have lost on points. There were accusations of corruption and dark hints that officials had been got at.

The main problem came, however, when another South Korean, a bantamweight called Jong-il-Byun, fought a Bulgarian, Aleksandr Hristov, in the Chamsil Stadium.

The referee was Keith Walker of New Zealand. He gave the Korean two public warnings for illegal use of his head. At the end of the bout the Bulgarian was declared the winner on a majority decision.

At this a number of South Korean officials, trainers and seconds decided to take a hand in the matter. Their chief boxing coach, Sung-eun-Kim, leapt into the ring and started shouting at referee Walker. He was followed into the ring by the Korean Chief of Security, a man called Yoon, who threw a punch at Walker. Other officials came to the assistance of the referee, who was pushed and pulled all over the ring.

More Koreans entered the ring to assist their coach and the security official. Some chairs were hurled across the ring and a bucket soared through the air. Eventually the ring was cleared of everyone but the boxer, Jong-il-Byun. He refused to leave. He squatted in one of the corners. He lay on his back. Some considerate person brought him a stool and he sat on that with great dignity.

Jong-il-Byun sat alone in the ring for over an hour, thus comprehensively beating the record of his fellow countryman Dong-Kih Choch, set in 1964, by seventeen minutes.

The Koreans on duty in the stadium staged a strike in sympathy with their compatriot. Someone even turned the lights out. The bantamweight sat on impassively.

At last Jong-il-Byun felt that honour had been satisfied. He rose from his stool, advanced to the centre of the ring, bowed gravely to the empty auditorium and left the ring.

Afterwards the authorities suspended the boxer's coach and a number of officials on the Korean team. Referee Walker caught the first aeroplane home. The President of the International Olympic Committee stated that he was heartily in favour of seeing boxing dropped from the Olympic programme.

The Security Chief, Yoon, who had hit the referee, later said that he had done so for the love of his country.

# The White Leather Jacket

## Harlem, New York, August 1988

Mitch 'Blood' Green, former New York Golden Gloves
champion, gang leader, street fighter and juvenile delinquent,
had been only the second fighter to take fearsome Mike Tyson
the distance during the latter's inexorable progress towards
winning the world heavyweight championship.

Tyson had been an easy winner of their ten-round bout at
Madison Square Garden in 1986, but Green had not been
impressed by the hype surrounding the young contender. He
had also been considerably annoyed by the fact that he had
received only $30,000 to Tyson's purse of $200,000.

The decision in favour of Tyson and the annoyances
connected with the bout rankled with Green, but they
retreated to the back of his mind as time passed. After all,
there were other things for the enterprising inhabitant of
Queens to be getting on with. Like having his driving licence
revoked more than fifty times, threatening to kill promoter
Don King, and commandeering a gas station by the simple
expedient of chasing away the attendant, selling the gasoline to
customers and neglecting to pass on the money to the garage
owner.

Life had not been uneventful for Tyson either. In the two
years since his Madison Square Garden bout with Green, he
had won the undisputed heavyweight title, splitting up with
his manager Bill Cayton, marrying starlet Robin Givens and
entering upon an extremely stormy relationship with her and

his new mother-in-law Ruth. Tyson had recently crashed his car into a couple of stationary vehicles in Manhattan and then given the $185,000 car to the two startled policemen who had arrived to investigate the accident.

The lives of the two fighters could not have been more different in August 1988. Tyson was wealthy, famous and besieged. Green had drifted back to the street corners. They met again in an odd way.

At four o'clock in the morning Tyson drove into Harlem to pick up a white leather jacket specially made for him at a clothing store known as Dapper Dan's, which remained open all night.

The sight of Tyson's Rolls-Royce outside the store attracted a great deal of local interest. Word reached Mitch Green that his former adversary was in the neighbourhood, and he hurried over to Dapper Dan's. He found the heavyweight champion inside the store collecting his jacket.

At once Green set about upsetting Mike Tyson. He opened the encounter by informing the champion that promoter Don King had robbed him by paying him only $30,000 for their Madison Square Garden bout. Apparently Tyson's reaction was not what the gang leader had been expecting. Green's accusation struck a chord with the champion.

'Don King robbed me too,' he allegedly agreed. 'He robs everyone.'

Green was disconcerted. While he was trying to figure out a response, Tyson left the clothing store. Green raced after him. His next approach was less subtle. He grabbed Tyson's shirt and tore it. He followed it up with a right hand to the champion's body.

It dawned on Mike Tyson that Green was not paying him a social visit. He hit his former opponent between the eyes, opening up a large gash. A brief scuffle followed before the two men were separated.

Mitch 'Blood' Green needed five stitches in the cut on his face. Mike Tyson had broken a bone in his right hand, forcing him to cancel a proposed bout with Frank Bruno in London.

Green sued Tyson for assault, but withdrew the charge

when he was presented with the inducement of a possible return bout in the ring with the champion. The catch was that Green had to get himself back into the top ten ranked heavyweight list before the fight could be sanctioned. He never made it.

# The Tartan Walk-Out

## Blackburn, April 1989

All over the world internecine strife has long been a fact of life among the administrators of amateur boxing. Officials from rival clubs treat one another with the utmost suspicion and unite only to condemn their national body. The different controlling organizations have about as much time for one another as the Montagues had for the Capulets on a bad day.

A fairly typical altercation between countries took place at the Amateur Boxing Association semi-finals for the British championships in 1989. The eleven members of the Scottish team spent little more than an hour at the hall before leaving without throwing a punch.

Two representatives from England and one each from Scotland and Wales had fought their way through to this stage of the ABA championships in the different weight classes. The two winners in each division would go on to the finals.

Before the bouts could get under way, the Scottish officials dropped their bombshell by announcing that they were withdrawing their whole team from the competition because the boxers were not allowed to wear protective headguards in the ring.

Spirited wrangling over procedural points went on for some time between administrators from the different nations. The Scots claimed that headguards had been declared compulsory at a recent international conference. The ABA officials countered by saying that the ruling did not apply to a domestic

236

championship such as theirs. Prevailing ABA rules would apply.

The Scottish officials shepherded their boxers back into the coach for the long journey home. Their champions had lost eleven contests without throwing a single punch.

# Mother's Boy

## Southampton, September 1989

Some boxing authorities forbid blood relatives to second a fighter, in case they become too emotionally involved. The strain imposed by watching a loved one fight – and getting beaten – was exemplified in the light heavyweight bout between two young British prospects, Tony Wilson and Steve McCarthy.

Wilson had the better pedigree of the two, having twice been British light heavyweight champion as an amateur and once as a professional. However, McCarthy seemed to be getting the better of their bout. He knocked the former champion down and then in the third round backed Wilson into a corner and started punishing him heavily.

This all proved to be too much for Tony's mother, Mrs Minna Wilson. She left her seat in the crowd, clambered up on to the apron of the ring, took off one of her high-heeled shoes and started belabouring McCarthy vigorously about the head with the implement.

Eventually order was restored and Mrs Wilson was persuaded to leave the ringside. At this point McCarthy discovered that he had sustained a cut on the head during his encounter with Mrs Wilson's shoe. He refused to carry on with the bout.

The referee then disqualified McCarthy and declared Wilson the winner. Although McCarthy's manager protested at the verdict, the British Boxing Board of Control upheld the referee's decision, but ordered the two fighters to meet again in their eliminator for the British title.

To McCarthy's relief, Mrs Wilson was banned from attending the return contest.

# *Boring!*

## Sheffield, January 1990

When Johnny Nelson of Sheffield challenged Carlos De Leon of Puerto Rico for the latter's WBC cruiserweight title, the prospect of such an intriguing contest and clash of styles had the fight fans in a crowded hall wondering what sort of bout was in store.

They were soon to find out. When the dreary charade was over the highly respected trade paper *Boxing News* described it as having been an inexcusable apology for a world title fight and an excruciatingly boring twelve-round draw.

In the cold light of day, many wondered if the magazine had been too flattering in its description. The Nelson–De Leon contest has a strong claim for the award of worst-ever world title fight.

There have been a number of other contenders. Several of Joe Louis's challengers were too terrified to strike a blow in anger, while both George Chip, a middleweight, and flyweight Frankie Genaro lasted less than two minutes in their championship bouts. Yet at least in these fights the spectators had the consolation of seeing the winners hit the losers quite hard.

The crowd at Sheffield should have been so lucky! De Leon was a cagey veteran who had survived forty-nine contests over a sixteen-year span by plodding patiently around the ring, adopting a safety-first policy and waiting for his opponents to make mistakes. By the time he came to Yorkshire, many

240

judges considered that the champion was ready to be taken by the first strong young fighter who could bustle him out of his stride.

Nelson was a gangling, engaging young fighter with a strangely unorthodox style. He would box with his arms at his sides, making sudden lunges at his adversary. His amateur record consisted of three wins in fifteen contests, while his professional career had seen him lose five out of twenty bouts.

For the entire twelve rounds of their title fight De Leon shuffled laboriously across the ring, his guard held high, trying to catch up with Nelson. For his part, the challenger fled around the periphery of the ring, scuttling backwards and occasionally licking out a long left hand. Usually he was out of distance. When he did connect it was mostly with the tip of his glove.

At first the spectators could not believe their eyes. As the terrible fight dragged on, with De Leon unable to connect and Nelson still offering his convincing impression of a pacific crab, they began to boo and give a slow handclap. When at last the referee demanded a higher work-rate from the fighters, there was a derisive cheer from the crowd but no discernible increase in the amount of action visible in the ring.

The fight eventually ended with both fighters sagging like run-down clockwork toys. The verdict of a draw caused no interest whatsoever.

Afterwards there was much criticism of the Sheffield fighter's approach to his big chance in the ring. His enraged manager said that he was fed up with the insults he had been receiving ever since the bout. He challenged any of his charge's detractors to come and work as Nelson's sparring partner, promising to pay the going rate of £700 a week.

The only response came from one disgruntled follower of the sport. He threatened to sue Nelson under the Trade Descriptions Act. The fan objected to Nelson's billing, which he used before every contest – Johnny, 'the Entertainer' Nelson!

# *Upset*

## Tokyo, February 1990

Iron Mike Tyson was the most fearsome and highly regarded heavyweight boxer of the 1980s. Even so, it took him three championship bouts before he was regarded as the undisputed champion.

This was because of the divided nature of professional boxing, with its different so-called controlling organizations.

In November 1986, Tyson knocked out Trevor Berbick in two rounds and was acknowledged by the World Boxing Council as the official champion. The following March he outpointed James 'Bonecrusher' Smith and was awarded the World Boxing Association title. In August 1987, he defeated Tony Tucker on points, and the International Boxing Federation accepted Tyson as the champion of the world.

When Tyson defended his title in Tokyo against James 'Buster' Douglas, both men assumed that the winner would be acknowledged as the champion. They were wrong, and the machinations which followed the bout revealed a great deal about what is wrong with professional boxing today.

Douglas was a 40 to 1 outsider, but he amazed everyone, including Tyson, by taking the fight to the champion from the opening bell. Tyson had broken with his trainer, Kevin Rooney, and manager, Bill Cayton, and did not look his customary swaggering self as the underdog stood up to his hardest punches and then launched his own furious attacks.

The only time that Tyson came into his own was in the

242

eighth round, when he managed to catch up with Douglas and knock him down for a count of nine. Afterwards, Tyson's backers claimed that the referee had been slow in taking up the count, and that the challenger had been on the canvas for some thirteen seconds.

The eighth-round flurry was Tyson's last contribution to the contest. In the tenth round Douglas knocked the champion out.

If Douglas thought that the hard part was over, he was in error. Almost as soon as Tyson had been helped out of the ring, the promoter and associate of the former champion, Don King, insisted that the result should be overturned because Douglas had really been knocked out in the eighth round.

King had strong links with both the WBC and WBA. Almost at once both organizations announced that they would not recognize Douglas as the new heavyweight champion until they had investigated all the circumstances surrounding the contest. The IBF declared that Douglas was the new champion.

The referee then claimed that Douglas had remained on the canvas too long in the eighth round because of the official's slowness in taking up the count. 'I am a man of honour,' he said. 'Unfortunately this is 100 per cent a human mistake.'

After a six-hour debate with colleagues, the president of the WBC announced, 'As of today, no one is heavyweight champion until 20 February when I meet with the WBC executive committee.'

'Truth should prevail,' said promoter King innocently. 'Fair play is all we're looking for.'

For a while, amid the confusion, it looked as if the new champion might be railroaded. However, the world's press came to his rescue. Newspapers in every country derided the fuss being made by Don King and the two controlling organizations. It became apparent that public opinion was strongly on the side of Buster Douglas. King announced that he, the WBC and the WBA all accepted Douglas as the victor over Tyson and consequently the new champion.

'The world recognizes James Douglas as the heavyweight

champion of the world,' said the fighter's manager John Johnson. 'He beat Mike Tyson's butt!'

As usual, the last word remained with the flamboyant Don King.

'I never asked anyone to change the decision,' he said self-righteously. 'We just want the first chance of a rematch!'

# Can Anyone Join In?

Birmingham, March 1990

Most fighters find it hard enough to contend with the opponent during a bout. Amateur welterweight Geoff McCreesh decided to take on part of the audience as well.

The occasion was the quarter-finals of the ABA championships at the Rover Exhibition Hall in Birmingham. McCreesh, from the Crownwood club, was fighting Robert McCracken of the City of Birmingham club.

The hall was filled with enthusiastic supporters and feelings were running high. At the end of the first round of the McCreesh–McCracken contest, a fight broke out between rival factions in the aisle. McCreesh saw that a relative was getting the worse of a struggle and dived out between the ropes to go to his aid, leaving McCracken, the referee and two sets of bewildered seconds in the ring.

The brawl raged up and down the hall, with McCreesh deeply involved. The MC appealed for decorum from the ring and begged the participants to return to their places. At last McCreesh came back into the ring and took his place on his stool, ready to resume his contest with McCracken.

He was disqualified for leaving the ring without the referee's permission.

# The Punching Promoter

## Lake Geneva, USA, June, 1990

The bane of any boxing promoter's life is the fighter who has to call off a bout because of an injury sustained in training. A fighter's build-up to a contest is handled very carefully indeed.

When promoter John Ellis matched former heavyweight contender Jerry Quarry against Paul Bradshaw, he set out to treat the big man with kid gloves.

Quarry had been out of the ring for some time, but still had a considerable reputation. He had been in with the best of them and had acquitted himself well against no fewer than three world champions – Muhammad Ali, Joe Frazier and Floyd Patterson. It was a considerable feather in John Ellis's cap to have signed up the former leading contender for his comeback attempt.

Unfortunately, all did not go well in training. There was a heated dispute over sparring partners and promoter Ellis had to be called in to settle the matter. Sharp words were exchanged between the heavyweight and the promoter. Before he knew what he was doing, Ellis had cocked his right hand and had let the disgruntled former contender have it right between the eyes.

The punch caused a gash on Quarry's face which needed nine stitches in order to close it. The proposed bout had to be cancelled – because of an injury sustained by Jerry Quarry in training.

# A Night to Forget

## Brighton, September 1990

Chris Eubank and Kid Milo did not gain a great deal of satisfaction from their middleweight bout at Brighton's Conference Centre. Neither did the spectators. However, the Brighton constabulary had quite a good evening, and so did an unknown burglar.

The contest got off to a bad start by being for the World Boxing Council's international title. This was one of the more synthetic championships in a sport littered with ersatz confections. The WBC's international titles were restricted to competition among boxers who were not rated in the top echelons of their divisions. Basically they were championships for boxers who were not good enough to be champions, which seemed to be carrying democracy a little too far.

The townsfolk of Brighton obviously shared this view, because the tournament was sparsely attended. The contest itself turned out to be a dull and bad-tempered affair. In hackneyed fashion, Eubank kept his challenger waiting in the ring alone while the champion's theme-song, 'Simply the Best', was played over the loudspeaker system. Eubank was on top throughout most of the bout, and eventually the contest was stopped in his favour in the eighth round, when Milo sustained bad cuts about his eyes.

The action when both contestants tried to leave the ring was far more exciting than anything that had happened during the fight. First Eubank became embroiled in a heated argument

247

with the flamboyant Ambrose Mendy, manager of world champion Nigel Benn. When Eubank tried to press his claim for a shot at the real title by hectoring Mendy, he found that he had more than met his match. Mendy delivered a torrent of cutting remarks at the middleweight, and finished by shouting triumphantly, 'Nigel will teach you how to fight and I will teach you how to talk!'

When it was Kid Milo's turn to leave the roped square, he found an even more intimidating reception committee waiting on the apron of the ring, in the shape of a posse of stalwart policemen.

Milo was arrested on the spot for failing to answer bail on charges of theft and criminal damage. Considerately the police took him to a local hospital to have his cut eye stitched before conveying him to Brighton police station.

If Eubank thought that matters could not possibly get worse, he was mistaken. When he got back to his hotel later that night he discovered that almost £7000 worth of jewellery had been stolen from his room.